THE MONK AND THE BUTTERFLY

Stories of Zen and The Art of Change

Kai T. Murano

Copyright © 2024 by Kai T. Murano
All rights reserved.
No portion of this book may be reproduced in any form
without written permission from the publisher or author, except
as permitted by U.S. copyright law
.

"Each morning we are born again, what we do today matters most."

— *Buddha*

Contents

	Introduction	1
1.	Zen and Mindfulness	4
2.	Zen and Positive Thinking	18
3.	Zen and Inner Peace	32
4.	Zen and Compassion	46
5.	Zen and Simplicity	60
6.	Zen and Adaptability	75
7.	Zen and Patience	89
8.	Zen and Letting Go	103
9.	Zen and Gratitude	118
10.	Zen and Connection	133
	Conclusion	147

Introduction

In the fast-paced world of today, where each moment rushes past us towards the next, there is a profound need for stillness, a space where the mind can breathe, and the heart can rest. This book seeks to be that space, a haven of tranquility and wisdom amidst the tumult of daily life, guided by the ancient and ever-relevant principles of Zen.

Zen, a school of Mahayana Buddhism, emphasizes the value of meditation and intuition rather than ritual worship or the study of scriptures. It teaches simplicity, directness, and the importance of personal insight. In its essence, Zen is not just a practice but a way of being, offering paths to mindfulness, inner peace, compassion, and enlightenment through its teachings and stories.

This collection of Zen-inspired tales is designed to illuminate the ten areas where Zen principles can profoundly impact our lives: Mindfulness, Positive Thinking, Inner Peace, Compassion, Simplicity, Adaptability, Patience, Letting Go, Gratitude, and Connection. Each section contains six stories, each a mirror reflecting the multifaceted truths of existence, inviting the reader to pause, reflect, and find wisdom in simplicity.

Through these stories, we will explore ancient Zen teachings in a contemporary context, drawing lessons that are as relevant today as they were centuries ago. The tales are not just narratives but gateways to contemplation, designed to guide the reader to moments of insight and understanding, to see the world and oneself through a lens of clarity and compassion.

As you journey through these pages, may you find the stillness you seek, the wisdom you crave, and the peace that has always been within you, waiting to be discovered. Welcome to a journey of discovery, of learning, and ultimately, of coming home to the Zen within.

"When walking, walk. When eating, eat."

— Zen Proverb

1

Zen and Mindfulness

In the rich tapestry of life, where moments weave together in a dance of light and shadow, Zen offers a path to clarity and presence. The journey into Zen and Mindfulness invites us to step into the fullness of each moment, to embrace life with an open heart and a keen awareness. This section of our exploration delves into the essence of mindfulness, a cornerstone of Zen practice, through stories that illuminate its transformative power.

Mindfulness, in the Zen tradition, is not merely a technique but a way of being. It is the art of being fully present in the here and now, of engaging with life as it unfolds, with a gentle, attentive gaze. The tales we present—ranging from "The Monk and The Butterfly" to "The Laughing Buddha"—are mirrors reflecting the myriad facets of mindfulness, each story a lesson in the subtle art of living consciously.

These narratives invite us to slow down, to breathe deeply, and to observe the wonder of existence in its simplest forms. They teach us that mindfulness is not a retreat from the world but a deeper engagement with it. Through the lens of mindfulness, every leaf becomes a scripture, every breath a prayer, and every moment an opportunity for awakening.

The stories in this section remind us that mindfulness is not confined to the cushion or the Zen garden but permeates every aspect of our lives. "The Tea Ceremony" reveals the beauty of mindful action, "The Mindful Fisherman" speaks to the peace found in presence, and "The Mountain Hermit's Silence" illustrates the profound quietude that comes from attentive listening.

Yet, the practice of mindfulness extends beyond individual tranquility. It fosters compassion, deepens our connection with others, and cultivates a sense of peace that radiates outward, touching all we encounter. As we walk the path of mindfulness, we discover that each step is a step towards greater understanding, kindness, and interconnectedness.

This introduction to Zen and Mindfulness is an invitation to embark on a journey of discovery. It is an exploration of how mindfulness can transform not just our own lives but the world around us. As you read these stories, may you find the space between breaths, the silence within sounds, and the tranquility within the tumult. Welcome to the mindful path, a journey of a thousand moments, each one an awakening to the beauty of the now.

THE MONK AND THE BUTTERFLY

In the heart of an ancient forest, where the trees whispered secrets of old, there lived a Zen monk named Liang. Monk Liang had devoted his life to the practice of mindfulness, seeking to live in the present moment, fully and completely.

One crisp morning, as the sun's rays pierced through the canopy, casting a mosaic of light and shadow upon the forest floor, Monk Liang sat in meditation beside a gently flowing

THE MONK AND THE BUTTERFLY

stream. His breath was slow and steady, his mind clear like the sky above, unmarred by the passage of clouds.

As he meditated, a butterfly, its wings painted with the vibrant colors of the forest, fluttered by. It danced in the air, carefree and graceful, eventually landing softly on Liang's knee. The monk observed the butterfly, noticing the intricate patterns on its wings, the delicate balance with which it held itself, and the subtle movement of its antennae.

In that moment, Liang was struck by a profound realization. The butterfly, in its simplicity and presence, was the embodiment of mindfulness. It did not worry about the past nor did it fear the future. It simply was, existing in the moment, fully engaged with the world around it.

Monk Liang smiled, a deep sense of peace settling in his heart. He understood that, like the butterfly, he too could live in each moment, fully and deeply, without attachment to the past or anxiety for the future.

From that day forward, Liang carried the lesson of the butterfly with him. He approached each task, each interaction, with full attention and presence, finding joy in the simplicity of being. To him, the butterfly had been a teacher, a guide back to the essence of mindfulness.

And so, the forest whispered a new secret, one of a monk and a butterfly, a tale of mindfulness and the beauty of living in the present. It was a lesson for all who walked its paths, a reminder of the peace that comes from simply being.

In "The Monk and the Butterfly" we are invited into a meditation on mindfulness, illustrating how peace and joy can be found in the simplicity of being. In observing the butterfly, Liang realizes that true mindfulness means engaging fully with the present, free from the burdens of past regrets or future anxieties. This story, set against the backdrop of an ancient, whispering forest, serves as a gentle reminder of the transformative power of mindfulness. It encourages us to embrace each moment with the same attention and presence as the butterfly, finding in this practice a path to inner peace and fulfillment. Through Liang's journey, we learn that mindfulness is not just a practice but a way of living, a lesson from nature on how to exist harmoniously within the world and with ourselves.

THE FARMER'S LOST HORSE

In a small village nestled between rolling hills and verdant fields, there lived an old farmer known for his wisdom and tranquility. One day, his only horse, which he relied on for plowing his fields, broke through the fence and ran away into the mountains. The villagers, upon hearing the news, rushed to the farmer's side, lamenting his misfortune.

"How unfortunate you are!" they exclaimed. "Now you have no horse to help with your fields. What bad luck!"

The farmer, unperturbed by the loss, simply replied, "Perhaps."

A few days passed, and to everyone's astonishment, the lost horse returned, not alone but accompanied by two wild horses it had befriended in the mountains. The villagers, amazed by the turn of events, gathered around the farmer once again.

"How fortunate you are!" they cheered. "Not only has your horse returned, but it has brought with it two more. What good luck!"

Again, the farmer responded with a calm, "Perhaps."

The next day, the farmer's son attempted to tame one of the wild horses. In the process, he was thrown off and broke his leg. The villagers, hearing of the accident, came to offer their sympathies for this stroke of bad luck.

"How unfortunate you are!" they said, shaking their heads. "Your only son, now injured. What bad luck!"

And the farmer, with the same tranquility as before, said, "Perhaps."

Not long after, a war broke out in the region, and all able-bodied men were conscripted into the army. Many from the village were taken, but the farmer's son was spared due to his broken leg. The villagers, now looking at the situation with new eyes, came to the farmer.

"How fortunate you are!" they exclaimed. "Your son's injury has kept him safe from the war. What good luck!"

The farmer, watching the changing seasons and the ebb and flow of fortune and misfortune, simply replied, "Perhaps."

"The Farmer's Lost Horse" teaches us the essence of mindfulness: living in the present without attaching ourselves to judgments of "good" or "bad" luck. Each event is a part of life's tapestry, interconnected and impermanent. By embracing the present moment as it is, we remain open to the flow of life, free from the suffering that comes with resistance and attachment.

THE TEA CEREMONY

In the bustling heart of Kyoto, there lived a tea master renowned not only for the exquisite tea he brewed but also for the mindfulness with which he conducted each tea ceremony. His name was Sato, and to him, the tea ceremony was not merely a tradition but a profound practice of presence and mindfulness.

One autumn afternoon, a troubled samurai visited Sato, seeking solace from the turmoil that plagued his mind. The samurai was accustomed to the ways of the sword, where action and reaction were swift, and patience was seldom a virtue. Sato welcomed the samurai into his tea house, a haven of tranquility amidst the chaos of life.

As the ceremony commenced, the samurai observed Sato's every move with a curious eye. Each action Sato took was deliberate and full of grace, from the gentle folding of the fukusa (silk cloth) to the precise whisking of the matcha (powdered green tea). There was a serene flow to his movements, a silent dance that spoke of years of practice and deep mindfulness.

The samurai, used to the fast pace of the battlefield, found himself slowing down, his breath syncing with the quiet rhythm of the ceremony. For the first time in many years, his mind was not racing with thoughts of battles past or anxieties about the future. He was here, now, fully present in the unfolding moment, captivated by the simple beauty of the tea and the warmth of the cup in his hands.

As they sipped their tea, Sato spoke softly, "In the way of tea, we find that now is the only moment we ever truly have. The past is a memory, the future a dream. But now, this moment – it is real, and it is ours to live."

The samurai, moved by the experience, found a peace he had long forgotten. The mindfulness practiced in the tea ceremony became a lesson he carried with him, a reminder that life, like the tea, is to be savored in the present, with attention and appreciation for the fleeting moments that make it whole.

"The Tea Ceremony," teaches us that mindfulness is not just a practice for the quiet moments of life but a way of being that can transform even the simplest of actions into a path to presence and peace.

THE MINDFUL FISHERMAN

In a quaint coastal village where the sea stretched to the horizon as a vast, shimmering mirror reflecting the sky, lived an old fisherman named Isao. Unlike other fishermen who took to the sea with haste at dawn, Isao approached his craft with a rare kind of mindfulness, treating each day as a unique dialogue with the ocean.

Isao's boat was small, and his nets were old, but his heart was full of gratitude for the sea's bounty. Each morning, as he rowed out into the dawn light, he did so with a quiet presence, observing the changing colors of the sky, the rhythm of the waves, and the dance of seabirds above.

One day, a young man from the city, burdened with the weight of his own thoughts and the relentless pace of life, came to the village seeking respite. He noticed Isao's serene approach to fishing and asked if he might join him, hoping to find some peace on the water.

Isao welcomed the young man onto his boat, and as they set out, he shared his philosophy of fishing—and of life. "The sea," Isao began, "is much like our minds. Some days it is calm and clear, and others it is stormy and opaque. But if we learn to be present with it, just as it is, we can find peace amidst both calm and storm."

As they cast their nets, Isao taught the young man to pay attention to the task at hand, to feel the pull of the net, the coolness of the sea air, and the gentle rocking of the boat. "Mindfulness," Isao explained, "is not about catching more fish, but about being fully engaged in the act of fishing. It's about being here, in this moment, with all your senses."

The young man, accustomed to a life of constant distraction, found the simplicity of fishing with Isao to be a profound experience. For the first time in a long while, his mind was not racing towards the next task or dwelling on past troubles. He was simply there, on the water, under the vast sky, alive to the world around him.

Through the mindful fisherman's example, the young man began to understand the value of presence. He saw that mindfulness could be practiced not just in solitude or meditation but in every act of daily life, from the mundane to the extraordinary.

"The Mindful Fisherman" teaches us that mindfulness is a way of engaging with the world with openness and curiosity, allowing us to find joy and peace in the simple act of being alive.

THE MOUNTAIN HERMIT'S SILENCE

High above a bustling village, where the air was crisp and the pines whispered secrets to the wind, lived a hermit known to the villagers as Master Hui. Nestled among the peaks, his life was a testament to the practice of Zen, particularly the profound silence and mindfulness it embraced.

Master Hui had once been a man of the village, involved in the daily cacophony of life below. But as the years passed, he found a calling in the silence of the mountains, learning the language of the wind, the trees, and the streams. His retreat into the mountains was not an escape from the world but a deeper immersion into the true essence of being.

One spring, a young woman from the village, Mei, sought out Master Hui. Plagued by relentless thoughts and the never-ending noise of her life, she yearned for peace. She had heard tales of the hermit who spoke the language of silence and decided to seek his guidance.

Climbing the mountain path, Mei found Master Hui sitting quietly outside his humble abode, his gaze lost in the distant horizon where the sky kissed the earth. Approaching him hesitantly, she asked, "Master Hui, how do you find peace in such silence? My life is filled with noise, and my mind is never still."

Master Hui welcomed her with a gentle smile, gesturing for her to sit beside him. They sat together in silence, watching the day slowly unfold, the sun casting golden hues across the sky, and the shadows playing among the rocks and trees.

As the hours passed, Mei began to notice the world around her in a way she never had before—the delicate sound of a leaf falling, the distant call of a bird, the whisper of the wind. In the absence of spoken words, she found a deeper connection to the world around her, a sense of peace that emanated from simply being present.

Finally, as the stars began to dot the sky, Master Hui spoke, "Silence is not the absence of sound, but the presence of an open heart. When we quiet the mind, we can hear the universe speaking through the language of existence."

Mei returned to the village with a new understanding. She realized that mindfulness was not about escaping noise or activity but about finding silence within, a calm center in the midst of life's storms.

"The Mountain Hermit's Silence" teaches us that mindfulness and peace are accessible not by removing ourselves from the world but by deeply engaging with it, moment by moment, with a heart open to the vast silence that holds all sounds.

THE LAUGHING BUDDHA

In a time when villages were scattered like pearls across a vast landscape, there was one who brought joy wherever he went—the Laughing Buddha, known as Hotei. With his enormous belly and jolly smile, Hotei wandered from village to village, a figure of happiness and the embodiment of mindful living.

Hotei carried nothing but a cloth sack filled with sweets, toys, and sometimes, just empty, symbolizing the simplicity and the surprises of life. He had no home, for the world was his dwelling, and every heart, his shelter.

One day, Hotei arrived at a village shrouded in gloom. The harvest had been poor, and the villagers were consumed by worry and despair, their minds fixated on the hardships of the present and the uncertainty of the future.

Seeing Hotei's joyful demeanor, a skeptical villager approached him and asked, "How can you laugh and be merry when life is so full of suffering?"

Hotei set down his sack, pulled out a candy, and handed it to the villager with a smile. Then, he began to laugh, his belly shaking like a bowl full of jelly. His laughter was infectious, and soon, a small crowd gathered, their curiosity piqued by this peculiar stranger.

Hotei pointed to his sack and said, "Life, like this sack, can seem heavy or light. It's not just about what it carries but how we choose to bear it. My laughter does not deny the pain of existence, but embraces the joy of being alive, here, now."

The villagers, initially puzzled, found themselves drawn into Hotei's laughter. One by one, their burdens seemed lighter, their worries less overwhelming. They began to see the beauty in their midst—the warmth of their community, the laughter of their children, and the simple pleasures that life afforded them, even in times of hardship.

Hotei's visit reminded the villagers that mindfulness is not merely the practice of solemn contemplation but also the celebration of the moment in all its facets. By being present, even in laughter and joy, one could find a profound sense of peace and contentment amidst life's inevitable challenges.

As Hotei left the village, his laughter echoing in the air, he left behind a lighter spirit and a message that would linger long after—mindfulness is the path to finding joy in the present moment, embracing life with a heart as open as his jolly laugh.

"The Laughing Buddha" teaches us that mindfulness and joy are deeply intertwined, inviting us to find contentment and laughter in the simplicity and beauty of the present moment.

REFLECTION ON LESSONS LEARNED FROM ZEN AND MINDFULNESS STORIES

The stories within the Zen and Mindfulness section, from "The Monk and The Butterfly" to "The Laughing Buddha," weave a narrative that underscores the profound simplicity and transformative power of mindfulness. Through these tales, we're invited to explore the depth and breadth of being truly present, and the ripple effects this presence can have on our lives and the world around us.

THE PRESENT MOMENT IS ALL WE HAVE

A central theme echoed across these stories is the paramount importance of living in the present moment. "The Monk and The Butterfly" teaches us that beauty, peace, and enlightenment are found not in the past or future, but right here, in the now. This story, like the others, encourages us to embrace the present with open arms and a keen awareness.

MINDFULNESS TRANSFORMS THE MUNDANE

"The Tea Ceremony" and "The Mindful Fisherman" illustrate how mindfulness can transform even the most mundane activities into acts of beauty, connection, and contemplation. These stories remind us that every action, no matter how small, is an opportunity to practice mindfulness, turning routine tasks into rituals of presence and attentiveness.

INNER PEACE THROUGH MINDFUL LIVING

"The Laughing Buddha" story highlights how mindfulness directly contributes to inner peace. By embracing the present moment with joy and openness, we can navigate life's challenges with a lighter heart and a clearer mind. This tale teaches us that mindfulness is not just a practice but a pathway to a more peaceful, joyful existence.

INTERCONNECTEDNESS AND COMPASSION

Mindfulness, as demonstrated in these stories, fosters a deep sense of interconnectedness and compassion. By being fully present, we become more attuned to the needs of others and the world around us. "The Monk and The Butterfly," for example, showcases how mindfulness opens our hearts, enabling us to act with kindness and empathy.

THE JOURNEY IS THE DESTINATION

Finally, these tales collectively affirm that mindfulness is a journey, not a destination. It's a continuous practice of returning to the present moment, again and again, learning and growing with each experience. The path of mindfulness, as shown through the lens of Zen stories, is one of constant discovery, an unfolding of the richness of life itself.

"THE MIND IS EVERYTHING.
WHAT YOU THINK, YOU BECOME."

-GUATAMA BUDDHA

2

Zen and Positive Thinking

In the vibrant mosaic of human experience, the power of thought stands as a pivotal force, shaping our perceptions, influencing our actions, and ultimately, crafting our realities. The Zen approach to positive thinking is not about naive optimism or ignoring life's challenges. Instead, it offers a profound understanding of how to embrace life with a mindset that acknowledges adversity while choosing to focus on the potential for growth, compassion, and joy. This section delves into the heart of Zen and Positive Thinking, unfolding stories that illuminate the path to cultivating a positive outlook grounded in deep wisdom and mindful practice.

Positive thinking, within the Zen tradition, is akin to planting seeds in a fertile garden. It is about nurturing thoughts that uplift and inspire, thoughts that are rooted in compassion, gratitude, and acceptance. The tales from "The Gift of Insults" to "The Lotus in the Mud" serve as parables for this journey, each story a reflection on the transformative power of maintaining a positive spirit even in the face of life's inevitable trials.

These narratives reveal that positive thinking is not a passive state but an active practice. It involves consciously choosing to see the light within the darkness, to find serenity amidst chaos, and to recognize that each moment, no matter how challenging, holds within it an opportunity for enlightenment. "The Two Wolves" teaches us about we have in nurturing positive or negative thoughts, that the wolf we choose to feed determines the direction lives.

Moreover, these stories emphasize that positive thinking is deeply interconnected with mindfulness. Through mindfulness, we become aware of our thoughts, allowing us to gently steer them towards positivity without attachment or judgment. "The Sunface Buddha, Moonface Buddha" illustrates this balance, showing how awareness of the present moment enables us to embrace both the joys and sorrows of life with equanimity and grace.

This introduction to Zen and Positive Thinking invites you on a journey of exploration, where the practice of positive thinking is not just a mental exercise but a way of being. It is about opening our hearts to the richness of the present, cultivating a mindset that embraces possibility, and walking through life with a deep sense of gratitude and wonder.

As you immerse yourself in the stories that follow, may you discover the seeds of positivity within you, ready to blossom into a life of profound joy, resilience, and peace.

THE GIFT OF INSULTS

In a small village nestled among the rolling hills, there lived a Zen master known for his unwavering calm and profound wisdom. His name was Master Kaito, and his presence was a beacon of peace in the bustling village life.

One day, a visitor from a distant land arrived in the village. Having heard of Master Kaito's reputation, the visitor sought to challenge him, to unsettle his serenity and prove that his calm was but a facade.

Finding Master Kaito in the village square, the visitor launched into a tirade of insults, each word sharper than the last, designed to pierce the armor of tranquility that the master was known for. The villagers gathered around, their breaths held, waiting to see how Master Kaito would respond to such provocation.

Master Kaito listened quietly, his expression unchanged, a gentle smile playing on his lips. As the visitor's words flowed like a bitter river, the master's calm remained unbroken, a rock amidst turbulent waters.

When the visitor finally paused, expecting a reaction, Master Kaito spoke softly, "If someone offers you a gift, and you choose not to accept it, to whom does the gift belong?"

Confused and taken aback, the visitor stuttered, "It... it remains with the giver."

"Exactly," Master Kaito replied, his voice calm and steady. "Just like your insults. You offered them to me, but I choose not to accept them. They remain yours."

The crowd was silent, the lesson clear. Master Kaito had not only maintained his peace but had also taught a profound lesson in positive thinking. He showed that our serenity does not depend on the actions or words of others but on our reactions to them. By choosing not to accept negativity, we retain control over our peace and happiness.

The visitor, humbled and enlightened by the encounter, bowed deeply to Master Kaito, thanking him for the invaluable lesson. From that day forward, the story of "The Gift of Insults" spread far and wide, a tale of the power of positive thinking and the strength of a peaceful mind.

THE TWO WOLVES

In the heart of an ancient forest, where the trees stood tall and wise, lived an old man known to all as the keeper of stories. One evening, as the fire crackled and the stars began to twinkle in the night sky, a young boy approached him, his heart heavy with anger and resentment.

"Grandfather," the boy said, "I feel as if there are two wolves fighting in my heart. One is full of anger, jealousy, and bitterness. The other is full of love, hope, and compassion. It frightens me, for I cannot tell which one will win."

The old man looked into the fire, his eyes reflecting the dance of the flames, and after a moment, he turned to the boy. "This battle you speak of is one that goes on inside every person, including myself."

The boy looked up, surprised. "But which wolf wins, Grandfather?"

The old man smiled softly, the warmth of his gaze enveloping the boy. "The one you feed," he replied gently.

"The one I feed?" the boy echoed, puzzled.

"Yes," the old man continued, "if you feed the wolf of anger and jealousy, with your thoughts, actions, and energy, it will grow stronger. It will consume you from the inside, leaving no room for peace or happiness. But if you choose to feed the wolf of love and compassion, nurturing it with kindness, understanding, and positive thoughts, it will flourish and fill your heart with light, driving out the darkness."

The boy sat in silence, contemplating the old man's words. He realized that the power to choose which wolf to feed lay within him. It was not a battle to be won by strength, but by choice—the choice of which thoughts to nurture, which feelings to cultivate.

From that day forward, the boy became mindful of the wolves within him, choosing to feed the wolf of love and compassion with every thought, every action. Over time, he found that the anger and bitterness that once troubled him had diminished, replaced by a sense of peace and happiness he had never known.

"The Two Wolves" teaches us the power of positive thinking and the importance of the choices we make every day. It reminds us that within us lies the ability to cultivate the qualities that lead to a fulfilling and joyful life.

THE SUNFACE BUDDHA, MOONFACE BUDDHA

In a monastery perched atop a serene hill, where the winds whispered ancient chants and the air carried the scent of incense, lived a Zen master named Ryūkan. He was revered for his deep understanding of Zen and the art of living in harmony with the universe.

One day, a disciple approached Master Ryūkan with a troubled heart. "Master," he began, "I have heard you speak of the Sunface Buddha and the Moonface Buddha. Yet, I find myself caught between joy and sorrow, hope and despair. How can I find the balance you speak of?"

Master Ryūkan invited the disciple to walk with him through the monastery's gardens, where the flowers bloomed in vibrant colors and the trees stood tall and steadfast.

"Observe," said Ryūkan, pointing towards the sky, "the sun shines brightly, illuminating the world, bringing warmth and light. This is the Sunface Buddha, the face of joy, vitality, and strength. Yet, the moon too has its beauty, serene and tranquil, reflecting light in the darkness. This is the Moonface Buddha, the face of calm, reflection, and peace."

The disciple listened intently as they continued to walk, the sounds of nature surrounding them in a peaceful embrace.

"Life," Ryūkan continued, "is an endless cycle of day and night, sun and moon, joy and sorrow. To embrace one and reject the other is to miss the fullness of existence. The Sunface Buddha reminds us to cherish the moments of happiness and strength, while the Moonface Buddha teaches us to find peace and reflection in times of darkness."

"Positive thinking," the master explained, "is not about denying the night in favor of the day. It is about seeing the beauty and learning in both, recognizing that each has its place in the cycle of life."

The disciple pondered Ryūkan's words, realizing that the balance he sought lay not in external circumstances but in his perception and acceptance of life's dual nature.

From that day on, he strove to embody the lessons of the Sunface Buddha and the Moonface Buddha, finding joy in the light and peace in the darkness, his heart no longer troubled but filled with the profound balance of positive thinking.

"The Sunface Buddha, Moonface Buddha" teaches us that positive thinking is about embracing all facets of life, finding balance and beauty in the ever-changing landscape of existence.

THE MIRROR OF THE MIND

In a bustling city filled with the clamor of daily life, there lived a wise old Zen teacher known as Master Enko. He was sought after by many for his insights into the nature of mind and reality. Among his many teachings, the concept of the mind as a mirror was one of the most profound.

One day, a young student troubled by negative thoughts and self-doubt came to Master Enko seeking guidance. "Master," he said, "my mind is always clouded with negative thoughts. How can I clear it and find peace?"

Master Enko led the student to a quiet room where a large, ancient mirror stood. The mirror was covered in dust and grime, reflecting a dim and distorted image.

"Look into this mirror," Master Enko instructed. "What do you see?"

"I see a blurred image, unclear and distorted," replied the student.

Master Enko handed the student a cloth. "Clean the mirror," he said.

As the student wiped away the dust and grime, the reflection in the mirror became clearer, revealing a bright and unobstructed image.

Master Enko then said, "The mind, like this mirror, reflects what is before it. If it is clouded by negative thoughts and doubts, the reflection we see is distorted. But if we clean it, if we cultivate positive thoughts and clarity, it reflects the world as it truly is, bright and unobstructed."

The student understood. The negativity that clouded his perception was not the reality, but a distortion created by his own mind. He realized that by practicing mindfulness and focusing on positive, constructive thoughts, he could clear the grime from the mirror of his mind, reflecting a brighter, truer view of the world.

From that day forward, the student devoted himself to this practice. As he became more adept at cultivating positive thoughts, his perception of the world changed. He found peace and clarity, even amidst the chaos of city life.

"The Mirror of the Mind" teaches us that our reality is greatly influenced by our thoughts. By choosing positive thinking and mindfulness, we can clear the distortions, seeing ourselves and the world around us more clearly and brightly.

THE PATH OF THE SUN

In a distant land where the mountains touched the skies and the rivers sang to the valleys, there was a path known to only a few. This path was said to be blessed by the sun, always bathed in light, never shadowed. It was here that a young wanderer named

Aiko found herself, seeking the enlightenment that had eluded her in the bustling cities and crowded markets.

Aiko had traveled far, her heart heavy with questions that weighed upon her soul. She had sought answers in the words of poets and the edicts of kings, but found no solace. It was said that the Path of the Sun held wisdom for those who walked its course, and so she followed, step by step, into the heart of the wilderness.

As she walked, Aiko noticed that with each step, the weight of her thoughts began to lift. The path, illuminated by the gentle warmth of the sun, invited her to cast aside her doubts and fears. She began to understand that the sun did not discriminate in its giving; it shone upon the just and the unjust, the strong and the weak, without judgment or hesitation.

This realization struck Aiko with the force of a revelation. She saw that the sun, in its endless journey across the sky, was a teacher of unconditional positivity. It did not withhold its light from the world because of the shadows; instead, it shone all the brighter, a beacon of hope and warmth.

Inspired, Aiko decided to embody the sun's lesson. She would strive to be a source of light and positivity, not deterred by the shadows cast by negativity and doubt. She understood that true enlightenment was not the absence of darkness but the presence of light, the choice to shine despite the shadows.

With this new understanding, Aiko's journey took on a different meaning. She no longer sought answers outside herself but became a seeker of light within. The Path of the Sun had shown her that positivity was not a destination but a way of being, a choice to walk in light, regardless of the darkness that may surround.

"The Path of the Sun" teaches us that positive thinking is akin to the sun's journey across the sky — a constant, unwavering force that illuminates our path, guiding us through darkness and doubt with warmth and light.

THE LOTUS IN THE MUD

In a serene valley surrounded by towering mountains, there was a clear, still pond. This pond was unlike any other in the valley. Despite the mud at its bottom, it was home to the most beautiful lotuses, their petals pure and untouched by the earth from which they grew.

A monk named Jiro lived near this pond. He was a teacher to many, known for his wisdom and the peaceful aura that surrounded him. One day, a traveler, weary from his long journey, came to Jiro seeking understanding about the nature of positivity and resilience.

Jiro welcomed the traveler and led him to the pond. They sat in silence, watching the lotuses sway gently in the breeze. Breaking the silence, Jiro spoke, "Notice how the lotus flowers bloom so beautifully above the mud. They do not disdain their roots in the murky water but rise above it, pure and unblemished."

The traveler listened intently, observing the flowers, a symbol of peace and purity amidst the darkness below.

Jiro continued, "Our lives, too, are much like the lotus. We may find ourselves rooted in the mud of difficulties and challenges. Yet, it is within our power to rise above these circumstances, to bloom with strength and beauty."

The traveler pondered Jiro's words, realizing the wisdom in the analogy. He understood that the mud, the hardships of life, was not something to be avoided or despised. Instead, it was the very thing that nourished and strengthened the lotus, allowing it to bloom so magnificently.

Inspired by this lesson, the traveler saw his own struggles in a new light. He recognized that positive thinking was not the absence of difficulties but the ability to rise above them, to remain pure and steadfast in the face of adversity.

As the sun began to set, casting a golden glow over the pond, the traveler thanked Jiro for his wisdom. He left the valley with a renewed sense of purpose, ready to embrace the challenges of his journey, just as the lotus embraces the mud from which it grows.

"The Lotus in the Mud" teaches us that true positivity comes from within, from the ability to rise above our circumstances and bloom with grace and beauty, no matter where we are planted.

REFLECTION ON LESSONS LEARNED FROM ZEN AND POSITIVE THINKING

The Zen and Positive Thinking section of our exploration weaves together a collection of stories, each shedding light on the profound impact of maintaining a positive outlook amidst life's ebbs and flows. From "The Gift of Insults" to "The Lotus in the Mud," these tales offer invaluable insights into the art of positive thinking as a transformative practice.

THE POWER OF PERSPECTIVE

A key lesson from these stories is the importance of perspective. "The Gift of Insults" illustrates that our reaction to external events—whether insults or setbacks—defines their impact on us. By choosing a positive perspective, we retain our power and peace, demonstrating that our internal response is our true locus of control.

THE CHOICE WE MAKE

"The Two Wolves" story vividly portrays the daily choice we face between fostering negative or positive thoughts. This tale reminds us that positivity is a choice, an active decision we make moment to moment. It underscores the responsibility we have in shaping our mindset and, by extension, our life's experience.

EMBRACING IMPERMANENCE WITH POSITIVITY

Zen teachings on impermanence are beautifully echoed in "The Sunface Buddha, Moonface Buddha," which encourages us to accept life's transient nature with a positive spirit. It teaches that joy and sorrow are part of the same cycle, and embracing both with a positive outlook can lead to a more balanced and fulfilling life.

MINDFULNESS AS A FOUNDATION FOR POSITIVITY

The practice of mindfulness, a recurring theme in Zen, is highlighted as a foundational element for positive thinking. Stories such as "The Mirror of the Mind" emphasize the role of mindfulness in recognizing and cultivating positive thoughts, allowing us to reflect a clearer, more joyful reality.

GROWTH THROUGH POSITIVITY

Finally, "The Lotus in the Mud" symbolizes the potential for growth and beauty even in challenging conditions, reminding us that adversity can be a fertile ground for development if approached with a positive mindset. This story encapsulates the essence of positive thinking in Zen—finding the lotus within the mud of our lives.

"Peace comes from within.
Do not seek it without."

— Buddha

3

Zen and Inner Peace

In a world where the noise of existence often drowns out the whisper of the soul, finding inner peace is both a journey and a destination. This section of our exploration into Zen stories delves into the heart of tranquility, through tales that illuminate the path to serenity amidst the storms of life.

Inner peace, as these stories will reveal, is not a state achieved by escaping the world's chaos but by embracing it with a calm heart and a still mind. The tales of "The Silent Mountain," "The Unfazed Flower," "The River's Flow," "The Monk and the Moonlight," "The Laughing Willow," and "The Reflection in the Pond" serve as guideposts on this journey, each story a beacon of light in the quest for harmony within.

The lessons of Zen, as presented through these narratives, teach us that inner peace is a reflection of how we engage with the world and ourselves. It is found not in the absence of noise, but in the ability to find silence within the noise. It is not the lack of conflict but the presence of a deep, abiding calm that flows beneath the surface of our struggles.

As we journey through these tales, we are invited to reflect on our own paths, to recognize that the quest for inner peace is a personal voyage. The stories serve as mirrors, reflecting back to us our own challenges and triumphs in the search for tranquility. They remind us that peace is not a distant land to be reached, but a place within us, waiting to be discovered.

Through meditation, mindfulness, and the wisdom of Zen, we learn to navigate the waters of our inner worlds, to quiet the storms that rage within, and to find the still point in the turning world. This section is an invitation to embark on this journey, to explore the depths of inner peace, and to uncover the serenity that resides within each of us.

Let these stories be your companions as you walk the path toward inner peace, each step an act of discovery, each breath a moment of mindfulness. Welcome to the journey within

THE SILENT MOUNTAIN

In a land of vast forests and towering peaks, there was a mountain said to be the abode of silence. Many sought its summit, hoping to find peace in the quietude that eluded them in the noise of their daily lives. Among these seekers was a young man named Taro, whose heart was burdened with unrest and whose mind was never still.

Taro embarked on his journey at dawn, the mountain's silhouette a dark line against the lightening sky. The path was steep, the air crisp, and with each step, Taro felt the weight of his thoughts, like stones in his heart, hoping that the summit would grant him the silence he so desperately sought.

After a day's climb, as the sun dipped below the horizon, Taro reached the summit. He sat, expecting a profound hush to envelop him, to wash away his turmoil. But the summit was alive with the sounds of rustling leaves, chirping crickets, and the distant call of birds. Taro frowned, his heart sinking. Where was the silence he had come for?

As night enveloped the mountain, a figure emerged from the shadows. It was an old hermit, his presence as serene as the moonlit landscape. Seeing Taro's distress, the hermit sat beside him and asked, "What brings you to the mountain's summit, young seeker?"

Taro shared his quest for silence, for peace from the tumult within. The hermit listened, then smiled gently. "The silence you seek is not the absence of sound, but the stillness of mind. It cannot be found on any mountain, but within you."

The hermit guided Taro in meditation, teaching him to observe his breath, to listen to the sounds of the mountain not as noise, but as music. Slowly, Taro's mind quieted, the stones in his heart growing lighter. He realized that the mountain's "silence" was not silence at all, but a symphony of nature, harmonious and beautiful.

With the hermit's guidance, Taro learned that inner peace was not the absence of noise, but the acceptance of it, the ability to find stillness within oneself regardless of the external cacophony. The true summit was not a place, but a state of being, a point of balance and tranquility within.

As dawn broke, painting the sky in hues of gold and pink, Taro looked out at the world below, a calmness within him that mirrored the serene expanse. He understood now that the silent mountain he had sought was, in fact, his own heart, silent and vast, waiting to be discovered.

"The Silent Mountain" teaches us that inner peace is not found in the quietude of the world around us, but in the silence we cultivate within, a lesson Taro carries back down the mountain, a treasure more valuable than any other.

THE UNFAZED FLOWER

In a small, tranquil Zen garden, amidst stones and sand meticulously raked into patterns representing the sea, stood a single flower. This flower, a bright chrysanthemum, bloomed with such vibrance and poise that all who entered the garden were drawn to its beauty. The garden was a sanctuary of peace, an embodiment of Zen, with each element carefully chosen to inspire serenity and reflection.

One evening, as dark clouds gathered overhead and a storm began to brew, a visitor found solace in the garden. She was a woman burdened with worries, her mind as tumultuous as the impending storm. Drawn to the solitary chrysanthemum, she marveled at how it stood so calmly, its petals undisturbed by the wind that rustled the leaves around it.

As the rain began to fall, gentle at first, then growing in intensity, the woman expected the flower to wilt under the onslaught. But as she watched, she saw the chrysanthemum bend gracefully under the weight of the water, only to rise again, its spirit unbroken, its beauty unmarred.

Intrigued, the woman sought the garden's keeper, an old monk known for his wisdom and the care with which he tended to the garden. She asked him about the flower, how it could remain so peaceful and steady amidst the storm.

The monk smiled, his eyes reflecting the calm of the garden. "The chrysanthemum," he began, "does not resist the storm. It does not fear the wind nor dread the rain. It simply exists, fully present in each moment, whether bathed in sunlight or drenched in rain. It knows that the storm is but a passing thing, and its essence remains unchanged."

The woman listened, the monk's words sinking into her heart. She realized that her worries, much like the storm, were transient, moments in the vastness of life that would pass. The flower's peace came from within, from an inner stillness that was not disturbed by the external world.

Inspired by the chrysanthemum, the woman began to see her challenges in a new light. She learned to embrace each moment, not as a struggle against the storm but as an opportunity to stand in her essence, calm and unfazed. The Zen garden, with its unassuming teacher, became a source of strength and tranquility, a reminder that inner peace is not the absence of conflict but the presence of inner harmony.

"The Unfazed Flower" teaches us that true inner peace comes from within, a serenity that endures through the storms of life, standing strong and beautiful in the face of adversity.

THE RIVER'S FLOW

In a verdant valley carved by time, a river wound its way through the landscape, a ribbon of blue amidst the green. Its banks were home to a small village, where the river was both a lifeline and a teacher. Among the villagers, there was a monk named Sojun, who often meditated by the river, finding in its flow a source of endless wisdom.

One day, a young man from the village, Kenji, approached Sojun. Kenji's heart was troubled, his life feeling as if it were a series of obstacles, each more insurmountable than the last. He sought Sojun's guidance, hoping to find a way to peace.

Sojun invited Kenji to sit with him by the river. "Watch the river as it flows," Sojun said, gesturing towards the water. "It meets rocks and boulders, yet it does not stop. It flows around them, over them, and continues on its journey."

Kenji watched, seeing how the water adapted, changing course with grace and ease. "The river does not cling to its path," Sojun continued. "It does not struggle against the obstacles. It embraces them, incorporates them into its flow, and moves forward."

"So it is with life," Sojun explained. "We meet obstacles, challenges that seem to block our way. But if we can learn from the river, to flow with the circumstances, not against them, we can find our way through with peace in our hearts."

Kenji pondered Sojun's words, watching the river. He saw now that his resistance to the challenges of life, his struggle against the flow, was what caused his turmoil. If he could learn to embrace the obstacles, to see them as part of his path rather than barriers, perhaps he could find the peace he sought.

In the days that followed, Kenji took Sojun's lesson to heart. He approached his challenges with a new perspective, seeing opportunities for growth and learning where he once saw only barriers. Like the river, he learned to flow with life, finding in its twists and turns a path to inner peace.

"The River's Flow" teaches us that inner peace comes from embracing life's challenges, flowing with them rather than resisting. It reminds us that the path to tranquility is not in the

avoidance of obstacles but in the acceptance and integration of them into our journey.

THE MONK AND THE MOONLIGHT

In a monastery nestled in the embrace of an ancient forest, where the trees reached up to brush the stars, there lived a monk named Hayato. Known for his deep contemplation and serene demeanor, Hayato often walked the monastery grounds by night, bathed in the silver glow of the moon.

One evening, a young novice, troubled by doubts and fears about his future, sought Hayato's counsel. He found the monk standing in a clearing, the moonlight casting a serene halo around him.

"Master Hayato," the novice began, his voice a whisper in the quiet of the night, "how do you find peace in a world of uncertainty? How do you remain so calm amidst the storms of life?"

Hayato turned to the novice, his eyes reflecting the calm of the moonlit night. "Come, walk with me," he said, leading the novice through the forest. As they walked, Hayato spoke softly.

"See how the moonlight touches everything with its gentle light, casting shadows yet revealing beauty in the darkness. The moon does not worry about the clouds that may hide it, nor does it fear the coming dawn that will outshine its glow. It simply shines, serene and steady."

Hayato paused, gesturing to the forest around them. "Like the moon, we too can find a peace that is not dependent on the absence of trouble or the presence of light. Inner peace comes from knowing that, like the moon, our light is not diminished by the darkness around us, nor by the clouds that may obscure it."

The novice listened, the monk's words seeping into his heart. He saw that his fears and doubts were like the clouds that pass across the moon — temporary, ever-changing. The peace Hayato spoke of was a tranquility that accepted the ebb and flow of life, that found steadiness in the self, regardless of external circumstances.

As the night deepened, the novice found himself looking at the moon in a new way. It was no longer just a celestial body in the sky but a teacher, its silent glow a lesson in serenity and acceptance.

"The Monk and the Moonlight" teaches us that inner peace is not a state to be achieved only in moments of stillness or solitude but a constant light within us, shining steady and serene through the clouds of doubt and the shadows of fear.

THE LAUGHING WILLOW

In the heart of a bustling city, there was a Zen garden, a pocket of tranquility amid the chaos. Central to this garden was a majestic willow tree, its branches swaying gracefully in the wind, leaves rustling with what sounded like laughter. This willow, known to the locals as the Laughing Willow, was not only a sight of beauty but also a symbol of peace and resilience.

A businessman named Hiroshi, weighed down by stress and the relentless pace of city life, found solace under the willow. Despite his success, he felt an emptiness inside, a yearning for a peace he couldn't seem to grasp.

One day, as Hiroshi sat under the tree, a Zen monk named Kaito joined him. Kaito was a frequent visitor to the garden, often seen meditating or tending to the plants with loving care.

Noticing Hiroshi's troubled expression, Kaito asked, "What brings you to the Laughing Willow?"

Hiroshi shared his struggles, how he felt adrift amidst his busy life, seeking but never finding inner peace.

Kaito smiled, gesturing towards the willow. "This tree," he said, "faces storms, strong winds, and the scorching sun. Yet, it stands tall and serene, its branches dancing with the breeze, laughing. It does not resist the wind; it flows with it, finds joy in the movement, the dance of life."

"The willow teaches us an important lesson," Kaito continued. "Inner peace does not come from a life without challenges but from embracing and flowing with these challenges. It's in the acceptance, the laughter amidst the storm, that we find true serenity."

Hiroshi listened, the monk's words resonating within him. He began to see his struggles not as barriers to peace but as part of the journey towards it. Like the willow, he could learn to bend and not break, to find joy and laughter in the face of life's winds.

Inspired by the Laughing Willow and Kaito's wisdom, Hiroshi's perspective shifted. He found himself engaging with his life's challenges with a new sense of grace and lightness, embracing the dance of existence.

"The Laughing Willow" **teaches us** that inner peace is achieved not by standing rigid against life's trials but by embracing them with flexibility and joy, finding the laughter that resonates through the storms.

THE REFLECTION IN THE POND

In the serene expanse of a Zen monastery, where the air was filled with the scent of incense and the sound of gentle chanting, there was a pond. This pond, clear and still, mirrored the sky above, a perfect reflection of the clouds, the flying birds, and the occasional leaf that fluttered down to touch its surface.

A warrior, weary from battles both external and internal, came to the monastery seeking peace. His heart was troubled, his mind clouded with the scars of war and the shadows of his past. He had heard of the monastery's wisdom and hoped to find solace there.

The abbot of the monastery, an old monk with eyes that reflected a deep understanding of the world's suffering and beauty, welcomed the warrior. Sensing the turmoil within the warrior's heart, he led him to the pond.

"Look into the water," the abbot said. "What do you see?"

The warrior saw his reflection, distorted by the ripples caused by his approach. "I see myself, broken and disturbed," he replied.

"Watch," said the abbot, and together they sat in silence, the air around them thick with the weight of unspoken thoughts.

As the warrior's breath slowed, and his heart quieted, the pond's surface returned to stillness. His reflection cleared, becoming whole once again, a perfect mirror of the world above.

"The pond," the abbot began, his voice soft yet carrying the weight of wisdom, "is like the mind. When agitated, it distorts and fragments. But when calm, it reflects the true nature of all things. Inner peace, like the clear reflection in the pond, comes from stillness, from calming the waters of your mind."

The warrior pondered the abbot's words, realizing that the battles he fought were not just against external foes but within himself. The peace he sought could not be won by sword or shield but by calming the tumult within.

In the days that followed, the warrior practiced meditation by the pond, learning to still the waters of his mind. With time, the reflection he saw each day grew clearer, not just the image of his physical form, but the reflection of a man at peace with himself and the world.

"The Reflection in the Pond" teaches us that inner peace is not found in the absence of conflict but in the stillness within. Like the pond, our minds can reflect the beauty and tranquility of the world when we learn to quiet the ripples of our thoughts.

REFLECTION ON LESSONS LEARNED FROM ZEN AND INNER PEACE STORIES

The stories within the Zen and Inner Peace section weave a rich tapestry of insights, each narrative shedding light on the multifaceted journey towards achieving tranquility in the midst of life's inevitable flux. From "The Silent Mountain" to "The Reflection in the Pond," these tales collectively underscore several core teachings of Zen, applicable to the contemporary quest for peace and balance.

EMBRACING IMPERMANENCE AND CHANGE

The stories remind us that change is the only constant. Like the river that flows around obstacles or the seasons that transform the landscape, embracing change rather than resisting it is key to finding inner peace. This acceptance allows us to navigate life's challenges with grace, understanding that each moment is transient and holds the potential for renewal.

FINDING STILLNESS WITHIN MOVEMENT

Zen teaches that peace is not found in stasis but in the movement and dynamism of life. "The Laughing Willow" and "The Monk and the Moonlight" illustrate how tranquility can coexist with the activity around us. By finding the still point within ourselves, we can maintain a serene heart, even as we engage fully with the world.

THE POWER OF MINDFULNESS

Mindfulness, the practice of being fully present in each moment, is a golden thread running through these stories. Whether it's observing the subtle beauty of a flower or recognizing the reflection in the pond, mindfulness allows us to experience life deeply, to appreciate the now without being overwhelmed by the past or future.

THE ESSENCE OF NON-ATTACHMENT

The lesson of non-attachment, beautifully illustrated by the flower that blooms amidst the storm, teaches us to hold our experiences lightly. By not clinging to specific outcomes or resisting what is, we open ourselves to the flow of life, finding peace in the acceptance of what comes and goes.

INNER PEACE AS A PRACTICE

Finally, these tales underscore that inner peace is not a destination but a practice. It requires conscious effort, be it through meditation, contemplation, or mindful living. Each story serves as a reminder that the journey to peace is ongoing, a path we walk every day with intention and awareness.

"IF YOU WANT OTHERS TO BE HAPPY, PRACTICE COMPASSION. IF YOU WANT TO BE HAPPY, PRACTICE COMPASSION."

— *DALAI LAMA*

4

Zen and Compassion

At the heart of Zen lies a profound emphasis on compassion, a boundless and unconditional kindness that extends to all beings. Compassion, in the Zen tradition, is not just a feeling but a way of living, an active engagement with the world that seeks to alleviate suffering through understanding, empathy, and love. This section, Zen and Compassion, unfolds stories that illuminate the multifaceted nature of compassion, exploring its depths through tales that inspire, challenge, and touch the heart.

The essence of Zen compassion is beautifully captured in the idea that we are all interconnected, that the happiness and suffering of others are intrinsically linked to our own. Through stories such as "The Monk and The Scorpion" and "The Blanket of Snow," we are invited to see the world through the eyes of others, to recognize our shared humanity, and to act from a place of deep empathy and kindness.

These narratives showcase compassion in action, highlighting the transformative power of extending kindness without expectation of return. "The Blossom of the Lotus" teaches us about the purity of compassion that blooms even in the most unlikely places, reminding us that our capacity for kindness is not diminished by the harshness of the world.

Furthermore, the tales of "The Gift of Water" and "The Hermit's Door" reveal that compassion often starts with understanding ourselves, with cultivating a gentle and forgiving heart towards our own imperfections. They underscore the importance of self-compassion as the foundation upon which we can build a more compassionate world.

Zen and Compassion also delves into the challenges of practicing compassion in a world that often seems indifferent or hostile. Stories like "The Broken Bird" confront us with the realities of pain and loss, yet also guide us towards finding strength in vulnerability and resilience in the act of caring.

This introduction to Zen and Compassion is an invitation to embark on a journey of the heart, to explore the depths of our capacity for kindness and to discover how compassion can transform not just our own lives, but the world around us. As we immerse ourselves in these stories, may we be inspired to live with a more open heart, to meet suffering with compassion, and to weave the threads of kindness into the fabric of our daily lives.

Through the practice of Zen compassion, we learn that every act of kindness, no matter how small, is a step towards a more compassionate world, a gesture of solidarity with all beings on the path of suffering and joy.

THE MONK AND THE SCORPION

In a quiet monastery nestled among lush hills and whispering forests, there lived a monk named Hoshin. Known for his deep understanding of Zen and unwavering compassion, Hoshin spent his days tending to the monastery's gardens and teaching the younger monks the ways of Zen.

THE MONK AND THE BUTTERFLY

One morning, while Hoshin was walking along the edge of a small pond within the monastery grounds, he noticed a scorpion struggling in the water, desperately trying to climb out but slipping back each time. Without hesitation, Hoshin reached into the water to lift the scorpion out. As he did so, the scorpion stung him, and he withdrew his hand quickly, but did not react in anger or frustration.

A young monk, who had been observing from a distance, rushed over. "Master Hoshin!" he exclaimed. "Why would you attempt to save the scorpion, even though it means harm to you?"

Hoshin looked at the young monk, a gentle smile spreading across his face. "Because," he replied, "it is the scorpion's nature to sting, just as it is my nature to save."

Undeterred by the sting, Hoshin used a leaf to carefully scoop the scorpion out of the water and set it safely on dry land. He then continued his walk, his steps as calm and measured as before.

The young monk, puzzled by Hoshin's actions, asked, "How can you show compassion to a creature that causes you pain? Does it not deserve to suffer for its actions?"

Hoshin stopped and turned to the young monk, his eyes soft but piercing. "Compassion," he said, "is not conditional. It does not depend on the actions of others, nor is it a currency for exchange. True compassion is understanding the pain of others and wishing to alleviate it, regardless of how they treat you. If I were to let the scorpion drown because it stung me, what would that say about my understanding of compassion?"

The young monk reflected on Hoshin's words, realizing that the lesson was not just about the scorpion but about the essence of compassion itself. It was a lesson in seeing beyond the immediate reaction to pain and understanding the deeper call to act with kindness and empathy, even when it's difficult.

"The Monk and The Scorpion" teaches us that compassion is a fundamental aspect of our humanity. It challenges us to act with kindness and understanding, even in the face of harm or misunderstanding, embodying the true spirit of Zen compassion.

THE BLANKET OF SNOW

In a small village shadowed by towering mountains, the arrival of winter was always a time of gathering, when the community would come together, sharing resources to ensure everyone's warmth and well-being through the cold months. One particularly harsh winter, the snow fell without cease, blanketing the village in a cold so deep it seeped into the bones of its inhabitants.

Among the villagers was an old Zen monk, Kaito, who lived in a modest temple at the edge of the village. Kaito was known for his deep compassion and wisdom, having spent many years in meditation and service to the community. As the winter grew more severe, Kaito noticed that some of the villagers, especially the elderly and the sick, lacked sufficient warmth, their thin blankets barely enough to stave off the cold.

One night, as the moon shone bright over the snow-covered village, Kaito took his own blankets—thick, woven with care over the years—and quietly left them at the doorsteps of those most in need. He did this in secret, asking for no thanks, desiring only to ease their suffering.

The next morning, the village buzzed with quiet surprise and gratitude for the mysterious gifts. When they discovered that it was Kaito who had sacrificed his own comfort for theirs, the villagers were moved by his act of selfless compassion. Inspired by Kaito's example, those who had extra blankets and warm clothing began to share with those who had none, weaving a web of kindness that warmed not just their bodies but their hearts.

As spring arrived, melting the snow and bringing life back to the village, the winter of shared hardships and compassion remained etched in the villagers' memories. Kaito's simple act of kindness had sparked a transformation, turning a season of suffering into a testament to the power of community and compassion.

"The Blanket of Snow" teaches us that compassion is often found in the quiet acts of kindness that recognize the interconnectedness of our lives. It reminds us that, like the blankets that brought warmth to the villagers, compassion has the power to envelop us in a shared humanity, strengthening the bonds that hold us together in the face of life's winters.

THE BLOSSOM OF THE LOTUS

In a bustling city filled with the noise of daily life, there was a small, forgotten pond. Once a place of beauty and tranquility, it had become polluted over the years, its waters murky, littered with trash, and devoid of life. Nearby, an old Zen temple stood, its presence a silent reminder of nature's resilience amidst urban sprawl.

The temple's abbot, a kind-hearted monk named Tadashi, would often sit by the pond's edge, meditating on compassion and the interconnectedness of all beings. He saw the pond not as it was, but as it could be—a sanctuary for life, reflecting the beauty of the sky above.

One day, Tadashi decided to act. With the help of his fellow monks and anyone willing to join, they began cleaning the pond, removing trash, and caring for the surrounding area. It was hard work, and progress was slow. Many passed by, indifferent, yet Tadashi remained undeterred, his compassion for the pond and its potential life unwavering.

As weeks turned into months, the pond began to transform. Clear water replaced the murkiness, and with it, life returned. Fish swam in the waters once again, birds visited, and plants flourished along its banks. The most remarkable change, however, came one morning when Tadashi discovered a single lotus flower blooming in the center of the pond—a symbol of purity and enlightenment, rising above the muddy waters.

The blooming of the lotus became a turning point for the community. Inspired by Tadashi's unwavering compassion and the visible transformation of the pond, people began to take notice. They saw the pond not just as a body of water, but as a reflection of their own actions and their capacity for change. The pond became a gathering place, a source of pride and beauty in the heart of the city.

"The Blossom of the Lotus" teaches us that compassion, when coupled with action, has the power to transform not just the physical world but the hearts of those who witness it. Tadashi's dedication to the pond mirrored the lotus's journey, a testament to the belief that from the murkiest waters, the purest beauty can emerge. This story reminds us that compassion is a force of nature, capable of bringing about real change, one act of kindness at a time.

THE GIFT OF WATER

In the heart of a vast desert, where the sun ruled with an unyielding blaze, there lay a small village. Life here was a testament to the resilience of the human spirit, with water more precious than gold, each drop a lifeline to the villagers.

Among the villagers was an old monk, Kenzo, who had made the desert his home many years ago. Kenzo had a small well, a hidden spring he had found and nurtured into a reliable source of water. While he needed little, he knew the value of his well to the village, especially in times of drought.

One day, a traveler, lost and near delirium from thirst, stumbled into the village. The villagers, wary of sharing their scarce resources, turned him away. But when Kenzo saw the traveler, he did not hesitate to offer him water, filling his flask and quenching his desperate thirst.

Grateful beyond words, the traveler asked Kenzo why he would share such a precious commodity with a stranger. Kenzo replied simply, "Water, like compassion, flows freely. To withhold it is to deny our very nature as human beings. We are all travelers in this world, and today, you were in need."

Years passed, and the traveler, whose life had been saved by Kenzo's compassion, found himself in a position of wealth and influence. Remembering the kindness shown to him in his hour of need, he returned to the village, not just with enough water to sustain them through the drought but with plans to build a system that would ensure no one in the village would ever suffer from thirst again.

"The Gift of Water" is a tale of compassion that transcends the immediate act of kindness. It speaks to the ripple effect of a single compassionate act, how it can grow and spread, transforming lives in ways we might never anticipate. Kenzo's act of giving water, a symbol of life itself, became a catalyst for change, turning scarcity into abundance.

"The Gift of Water" teaches us that compassion is not just an emotional response but a practical expression of our interconnectedness. Just as water connects every living thing, so too does compassion link us all, reminding us that in helping others, we nourish the very essence of humanity.

THE HERMIT'S DOOR

In a dense forest that seemed to hold its breath under the weight of the world, there was a small clearing where an old hermit lived in a humble hut. The hermit, known as Master Sato, had spent many years in solitude, dedicating his life to meditation and the understanding of Zen. Despite his seclusion, tales of his wisdom and compassion had spread far and wide.

One bitterly cold winter's night, as the wind howled like the cries of lost spirits, there came a knock at the hermit's door. Master Sato opened it to find a shivering stranger, a young man whose eyes held the desperation of someone who had nowhere else to turn.

Without a word, Master Sato welcomed the stranger inside, offering him the warmth of his fire and the little food he had. The young man, overwhelmed by the hermit's kindness, asked, "Why do you open your door to a stranger like me? How do you know I won't harm you or take advantage of your generosity?"

Master Sato, tending to the fire, replied, "The door of compassion is never closed, for to live in fear of being harmed or taken advantage of is to close off our hearts to the very essence of life. We are all travelers on a journey, and tonight, your journey needed warmth and shelter."

The young man, moved by the hermit's words, shared his story of loss and hardship, of how he had come to be so far from home without food or shelter. As the night deepened, Master Sato listened, his presence a comforting balm to the young man's troubled heart.

By morning, the storm had passed, and the young man prepared to leave. Before he did, Master Sato handed him a small pouch of food and a flask of water. "Take these," he said, "for the road ahead may still hold challenges. Remember, the compassion you've received here is not just for you to keep, but to share with those you meet along your way."

The young man left, his heart lighter, not just from the physical warmth and nourishment he had received, but from the warmth of compassion that had touched his soul. In time, he would come to understand the depth of Master Sato's lesson: that compassion, once kindled in the heart, is a flame meant to be passed on, illuminating the path not just for ourselves but for others as well.

"The Hermit's Door" teaches us that compassion is an open door, a choice to extend kindness and understanding even when we have little to give. It reminds us that the true measure of our humanity lies not in our wealth or status, but in our willingness to open our hearts to others, especially those in need.

THE BROKEN BIRD

In the outskirts of a bustling village, where the hustle of daily life seldom slowed, a young girl named Miya found a bird with a broken wing. The bird, a small sparrow, trembled in the cold, its eyes filled with fear. Miya, whose heart was as tender as the morning dew, could not bear to leave the bird to fend for itself.

She carefully picked up the sparrow and brought it home. There, Miya created a warm nest out of an old shoebox, feeding the bird and tending to its wing with gentle hands. Each day, she would speak to the bird in soft whispers, offering words of encouragement and kindness.

As days turned into weeks, the sparrow began to heal. Its wing, once fragile and bent, grew stronger, and its eyes sparkled with a newfound zest for life. Miya watched with joy as the bird took its first tentative flight around her room.

The time came for the sparrow to return to the wild. Miya, though saddened by the thought of parting with her feathered friend, knew that the greatest act of compassion she could offer was to let the bird fly free. On a bright morning, with the sun casting golden hues across the sky, Miya opened her window and watched as the sparrow soared into the blue, its spirit unbroken.

Moved by Miya's selfless act of kindness, the villagers, who had learned of her care for the bird, began to see the world around them with new eyes. They noticed the beauty of the life that thrived in their midst, the interconnectedness of all beings, and the power of compassion to heal and transform.

"The Broken Bird" teaches us that compassion, in its purest form, is an act of unconditional love and release. It is understanding that true kindness sometimes means letting go, allowing others to find their own strength and path. Miya's story is a reminder that even the smallest acts of compassion can have a profound impact, not just on those we help but on ourselves and our community.

"The Broken Bird" teaches us that compassion is not just a feeling but a way of being in the world, a gentle touch that mends broken wings and spirits, inspiring others to spread their own wings and fly.

REFLECTION ON LESSONS LEARNED FROM ZEN AND COMPASSION STORIES

THE UNIVERSALITY OF COMPASSION

The stories collectively teach that compassion knows no bounds. It extends beyond human interactions to encompass all living beings, as illustrated by the monk's unwavering kindness towards the scorpion. This universality underscores a fundamental Zen teaching: all life is interconnected, and our actions ripple through this web of existence.

COMPASSION AS A FORM OF ACTION

Zen and Compassion stories emphasize that true compassion is active, not passive. It's about taking concrete steps to alleviate suffering, whether through a simple act of kindness, like sharing water in "The Gift of Water," or through more significant efforts to change a community's circumstances, as seen in "The Blanket of Snow." Compassion, therefore, is not just an emotional state but a call to action.

THE RIPPLE EFFECT OF COMPASSION

"The Gift of Water" and "The Hermit's Door" highlight the expansive impact of compassionate acts. A single gesture of kindness can inspire others, creating a domino effect that transforms communities and, potentially, society at large. This ripple effect underscores the power of compassion to initiate change, encouraging us to consider how our actions might inspire kindness in others.

COMPASSION AND SELF-TRANSFORMATION

Engaging in acts of compassion not only benefits others but also transforms the individual practicing it. Stories like "The Broken Bird" and "The Blossom of the Lotus" illustrate how caring for others cultivates a sense of fulfillment, purpose, and connection, enriching the giver's life. This self-transformation is a crucial aspect of Zen practice, where personal growth and enlightenment are intertwined with compassionate living.

COMPASSION AS A PATH TO ENLIGHTENMENT

Finally, these stories suggest that compassion is a path to enlightenment. By putting the well-being of others before our own, we break down the ego and open our hearts, moving closer to a state of oneness with all beings. This path is beautifully symbolized in "The Blossom of the Lotus," where the act of cleaning a pond not only purifies the water but also the hearts of those involved.

"Simplicity is the ultimate sophistication."

— Leonardo da Vinci

5

Zen and Simplicity

In the intricate tapestry of life, where complexity often clouds our vision and burdens our hearts, Zen calls us back to the essence of simplicity. This ancient wisdom teaches that in stripping away the superfluous, we uncover the true richness of life. The Zen and Simplicity section unfolds through stories that embody this principle, guiding us to find beauty in the mundane, peace in stillness, and depth in the ordinary.

Simplicity in Zen is not merely about minimalism or the absence of clutter but a profound realization of what truly matters. It's about seeing the world more clearly, unobstructed by our endless desires and distractions. Through tales like "The Empty Cup" and "The Wooden Bowl," we are invited to discover the freedom and joy that come from living with less.

These narratives challenge us to reconsider our values and the way we interact with the world. They teach us that simplicity is not a sacrifice but a path to liberation, offering a counter-narrative to a culture consumed by accumulation and excess.

As we journey through these stories, we're encouraged to apply the lessons of simplicity to our own lives. Whether it's through decluttering our physical spaces, simplifying our daily routines, or cultivating a mindset that values presence over productivity, the practice of simplicity offers a gateway to a more mindful, contented existence.

In embracing simplicity, we also find a deeper connection to nature, to each other, and to ourselves. Zen and Simplicity stories, such as "The Mountain Path" and "The Monk's Belongings," illuminate this interconnectedness, reminding us that in simplicity, we find our common humanity and our place within the natural world.

This introduction to Zen and Simplicity invites you on a journey of discovery, where less truly becomes more, and where the simplest acts and moments become the most profound. Let these stories be a guide back to the essence, a reminder of the peace and clarity that simplicity brings.

THE EMPTY CUP

In a quaint village where the mountains met the sky, and the rivers sang lullabies, there lived an old Zen master, known for his wisdom and serene way of life. His name was Master Kaito, and he had spent many years cultivating a garden of enlightenment, not only around his modest hut but within his soul.

One day, a young scholar from the city, eager to learn the secrets of Zen, sought out Master Kaito. The scholar had read many books and attended numerous lectures, his mind brimming with knowledge. He arrived at the master's hut, his cup of tea metaphorically overflowing.

Master Kaito welcomed the scholar with a gentle nod and invited him to sit for tea. As Kaito prepared the tea with deliberate and mindful actions, the scholar began to speak of all he had learned, pouring out his theories and insights on Zen, barely pausing for breath.

Master Kaito listened quietly, a slight smile playing on his lips. Once the tea was ready, he began to pour it into the scholar's cup. The tea rose to the brim, but Kaito kept pouring. The tea spilled over, streaming onto the table and dripping onto the floor.

"Master Kaito!" exclaimed the scholar, finally pausing in his monologue. "The cup is overflowing; no more will go in!"

Master Kaito placed the teapot down and met the scholar's eyes. "Like this cup," he said softly, "you are full of your own opinions and speculations. How can I show you Zen unless you first empty your cup?"

The scholar sat in stunned silence, the truth of Master Kaito's words washing over him like the spilled tea. He realized that his pursuit of knowledge had become clutter, a barrier to truly understanding Zen. In that moment, he felt a shift within him, a space opening up.

The following days, the scholar spent in quiet reflection, observing Master Kaito's simple way of life, the mindful attention to each task, and the profound peace that filled the master's modest hut. Gradually, the scholar learned to empty his cup, letting go of preconceived notions and the need to fill the silence with words.

In the simplicity of silence, in the act of emptying his cup, the scholar found the essence of Zen. It was not in the accumulation of knowledge but in the presence of being, in the clear space of an empty cup, ready to receive the tea, ready to receive life.

"The Empty Cup" teaches us that simplicity and openness are the keys to wisdom. It reminds us that to truly learn and grow, we must be willing to let go, to empty our cups, and to approach life with a heart ready to receive the simple, profound truths of existence.

THE MONK'S BELONGINGS

In a remote monastery perched atop a serene hill, there lived a monk named Hideo. Hideo had spent many years in the monastery, his life a testament to the practice of Zen and the 333333333pursuit of simplicity. Over the years, however, Hideo had accumulated a modest collection of possessions, each carrying a memory, a lesson, or a gift from a fellow monk.

One spring, as Hideo cleaned his small living quarters, he paused to consider each item he owned. He realized that, despite their sentimental value, many of his possessions were rarely used. They filled his space, not with joy, but with a quiet clutter that had, over time, become a subtle burden.

Inspired by a teaching of Master Kaito about the beauty of emptiness and the freedom found in simplicity, Hideo made a decision. He would keep only what was necessary for his daily life and practice, releasing the rest with gratitude for the role each item had played in his journey.

Hideo began with his books, many of which he had read and learned from but now sat gathering dust. He chose to donate them to the village library, where they could continue to enlighten others. Next were the garments and trinkets, gifts from visitors and friends, which he offered to the monastery's guests and to the villagers.

With each item Hideo let go, he felt a weight lifting. His quarters became more open, filled with light and air. There was beauty in the emptiness, a serene landscape that mirrored the inner peace he sought in his practice.

But the true test came when Hideo considered his most cherished possession, a small, intricately carved wooden Buddha, a gift from his late master. It had been a constant companion in his practice, a symbol of his commitment to the path. After much contemplation, Hideo understood that the essence of Buddha was not in the carving but in his heart. With a deep sense of peace, he placed the statue in the monastery's main hall, where it could inspire all who entered.

"The Monk's Belongings" is a story of letting go, of finding freedom in simplicity, and of the profound peace that comes from embracing emptiness. Hideo's journey teaches us that our possessions, while meaningful, do not define us. True richness lies in the simplicity of life, in the space we create for peace, mindfulness, and the unfettered pursuit of enlightenment.

Through Hideo's example, we learn that simplicity is not just a physical practice but a spiritual one, offering a path to a deeper understanding of ourselves and the world around us.

THE SIMPLE MEAL

In the heart of a bustling city, where the days were marked by the endless pursuit of more, lived a wealthy merchant named Akio. His life was a testament to his success, filled with luxurious possessions and extravagant meals. Yet, amidst this abundance, Akio felt an unshakable sense of emptiness, a hunger that no material wealth could satisfy.

Seeking wisdom, Akio visited a Zen monastery nestled in a tranquil forest on the city's outskirts. There, he was welcomed by an elderly monk, Master Sato, who lived a life of profound simplicity. Akio was intrigued by the monk's serene demeanor and the stark contrast between their ways of life.

Master Sato invited Akio to join him for a meal. Expecting a feast befitting his status, Akio was surprised when presented with a simple meal of rice, vegetables, and tea. The simplicity of the food, served on plain, unadorned pottery, was a far cry from the lavish meals Akio was accustomed to.

As they ate, Master Sato spoke of the Zen principle of simplicity, how it clears the mind and opens the heart. "In each grain of rice, in every leaf of the vegetable, there is a universe," he said. "When we eat with mindfulness and gratitude, even the simplest meal becomes a feast."

Akio listened, his initial disappointment giving way to a growing sense of awareness. With each bite, he began to taste more than just the food; he tasted the labor that brought it to the table, the earth that nourished it, and the interconnectedness of all things. The meal, simple in its ingredients yet rich in its essence, filled him in a way no luxury ever had.

The experience was a revelation to Akio. He realized that his pursuit of material wealth had led him away from the very essence of life. The emptiness he felt was not a void to be filled with possessions but a space for simplicity, mindfulness, and true connection.

Moved by the meal and Master Sato's wisdom, Akio began to incorporate simplicity into his own life. He found joy in the ordinary, richness in minimalism, and an abundance of spirit in the act of giving. The simple meal at the monastery had nourished not just his body but his soul, teaching him that the essence of fulfillment lies not in having more, but in being fully present with less.

"The Simple Meal" is a story of transformation, a reminder that simplicity offers a path to a deeper understanding and appreciation of life. It invites us to reconsider what we value, to find beauty in the mundane, and to discover that in simplicity, there lies a profound depth of richness and satisfaction.

THE PAPER CRANE

In a small village where tradition and modernity intertwined like the threads of an old tapestry, there lived a young girl named Hina. Amidst the hustle of daily life, Hina's world was one of simplicity and joy, largely untouched by the complexities that filled the lives of those around her. Her greatest treasure was a piece of paper, smooth and white, a canvas for her imagination.

One day, while exploring the edges of the village, Hina encountered an old Zen monk named Takahiro. Takahiro was sitting under the shade of a cherry blossom tree, his eyes closed in meditation, a picture of peace. Curious, Hina approached quietly, not wanting to disturb the tranquil scene.

As Takahiro opened his eyes, he noticed Hina's wide-eyed curiosity. With a gentle smile, he invited her to sit beside him. He asked about the piece of paper she clutched tightly in her hand. Hina explained that she loved to draw and fold paper, creating shapes and figures from her imagination.

Seeing an opportunity to teach a valuable lesson, Takahiro asked if he might show her how to make a paper crane. Hina nodded eagerly, her interest piqued. Takahiro took the paper and, with slow, deliberate folds, transformed it into a beautiful crane. The simplicity of the action, the transformation of a plain piece of paper into something so elegant and full of life, left Hina in awe.

Takahiro then shared the significance of the paper crane in Japanese culture as a symbol of peace, healing, and hope. He spoke of the importance of simplicity, of finding joy in the small, quiet acts of creation. "Simplicity," he said, "is the key to uncovering the beauty hidden in the ordinary, to connecting with the deeper rhythms of life."

Hina listened intently, the paper crane now resting in her palm. She realized that the joy she found in her paper creations was not about the complexity of the designs but the love and imagination that went into them. It was a lesson in mindfulness, in being fully present in the moment of creation, appreciating the simple pleasure of folding paper.

Inspired by Takahiro's words and the elegance of the paper crane, Hina began to approach her craft with a new perspective. She saw her paper not as a means to an end but as a path to mindfulness and simplicity, a way to connect with the world around her in a deeper, more meaningful way.

"The Paper Crane" teaches us that simplicity can be a source of profound joy and inspiration. It reminds us that in the act of creating, in the appreciation of the simple and the mundane, we find a connection to the essence of life, a peace that transcends the need for more and speaks to the heart of being.

THE ZEN GARDEN

In a bustling city where the pace of life never seemed to slow, there existed a small Zen garden, an oasis of tranquility amidst the chaos. This garden was tended by an elderly monk named Isao, who had dedicated his life to maintaining its beauty and simplicity. The garden was not grand or filled with colorful flowers but was composed of rocks, sand, and a few carefully pruned plants, each element placed with intention and mindfulness.

A young architect named Emiko, known for her innovative and complex designs, stumbled upon this garden one day. She was immediately struck by its stark simplicity and the profound sense of peace that enveloped her as she walked its paths. Curious, she sought out Isao, hoping to understand the philosophy behind the garden's design.

Isao welcomed Emiko's interest and shared with her the principles of Zen gardening, explaining how each element of the garden represented a part of the natural world and how the empty spaces were just as important as the elements that filled them. "Simplicity," he said, "is not about the absence of complexity but about the harmony and balance that arises when every part serves a purpose."

Emiko was intrigued. She had always believed that more was better, that complexity in her designs equated to creativity and innovation. Yet, the Zen garden challenged her beliefs, showing her that simplicity could convey depth and meaning in a way she had never considered.

Inspired by Isao and the garden, Emiko began to explore the concept of simplicity in her own work. She experimented with reducing her designs to their essential elements, focusing on balance and harmony rather than adornment and excess. This new approach was met with acclaim, her projects resonating with a sense of calm and clarity that reflected the principles of the Zen garden.

Through her journey, Emiko learned that simplicity is a form of wisdom, a way of seeing the beauty in the minimal and the understated. The Zen garden, with its rocks, sand, and sparse vegetation, taught her that true elegance lies in the quiet confidence of knowing that nothing is superfluous, that everything has its place.

"The Zen Garden" is a story of discovery and transformation. It teaches us that the principles of Zen and simplicity can extend beyond the garden and into every aspect of our lives, offering a path to clarity and peace in a world that often values complexity and noise. It reminds us that in the simplicity of a Zen garden, as in life, there is a profound beauty and a deep connection to the essence of the world around us.

THE WEAVER'S LOOM

In a village where the mountains kissed the clouds, there lived a weaver named Aiko. Her loom was old and simple, a family heirloom passed down through generations. Unlike the modern machines that filled the factories in the city, Aiko's loom required patience, skill, and a mindful presence. Each thread was woven with intention, creating patterns that told stories of the village, its people, and the land that nurtured them.

Aiko's work was a meditation, her movements synchronized with the rhythmic clacking of the loom. To the untrained eye, her task seemed monotonous, the simplicity of the loom a limitation. Yet, Aiko found joy and profound fulfillment in her craft. Each piece she created was a testament to the beauty of simplicity, a reflection of the world around her distilled into its essence.

One day, a businessman from the city visited Aiko's workshop. He was fascinated by her skill and offered to buy her creations, suggesting she could make more money with a modern loom. Aiko listened politely but declined. "The value of my work," she explained, "is not measured by the speed at which I produce or the money I make. It lies in the connection I feel to each thread, to the stories I weave, and to the tradition I uphold."

The businessman, accustomed to a world where efficiency and profit were paramount, was taken aback. He watched Aiko at her loom, noting the care she took with each thread, the way her creations came to life under her skilled hands. As he observed, he began to understand. Aiko's approach to weaving was not just about making textiles; it was a practice of Zen simplicity, a way of life that embraced the richness of doing less but with greater depth and meaning.

Moved by the experience, the businessman left the village with a new perspective. He carried with him not just one of Aiko's textiles but the lesson of the weaver's loom—a reminder that in the pursuit of simplicity, we find clarity, purpose, and a deeper connection to the essence of our work and lives.

"The Weaver's Loom" teaches us that simplicity is not a limitation but a foundation for creativity, mindfulness, and connection. It invites us to look beyond the surface, to find joy and meaning in the process, and to appreciate the beauty and richness that simplicity brings to our lives.

REFLECTION ON LESSONS LEARNED FROM ZEN AND SIMPLICITY

EMBRACING SIMPLICITY AS A PATH TO CLARITY

The Zen and Simplicity stories collectively underscore the clarity that simplicity brings to our lives. "The Empty Cup" teaches us the importance of approaching life with an openness to learn and grow, free from the clutter of preconceived notions. This clarity of mind, akin to the clear surface of an undisturbed pond, allows us to perceive the depth and richness of our experiences with renewed insight.

THE JOY FOUND IN MINDFUL ENGAGEMENT

Through "The Paper Crane" and "The Weaver's Loom," we learn that simplicity fosters a deep, joyful engagement with the tasks at hand. This mindful engagement transforms ordinary activities into meditative practices, revealing the inherent beauty and satisfaction in the act of creation. Simplicity, therefore, becomes a conduit for mindfulness, inviting us to fully immerse ourselves in the present moment.

LETTING GO AS AN ACT OF FREEDOM

"The Monk's Belongings" illustrates the liberating power of letting go. By releasing our attachment to material possessions, we free ourselves from the burdens that weigh down our spirit. This act of letting go is not a loss but a gain, creating space for peace, freedom, and a deeper appreciation for what truly matters.

THE INTERCONNECTEDNESS OF SIMPLICITY AND NATURE

Stories like "The Zen Garden" remind us of the intrinsic connection between simplicity and the natural world. The careful arrangement of rocks and sand in a Zen garden mirrors the simplicity and balance found in nature, teaching us to cultivate harmony in our surroundings and within ourselves. This interconnectedness encourages a respectful, mindful coexistence with the natural world.

SIMPLICITY AS A FOUNDATION FOR CONTENTMENT

Across the Zen and Simplicity narratives, there is a recurring theme of contentment found in living simply. This contentment is not rooted in complacency but in a profound appreciation for the present and the essentials of life. Simplicity, therefore, is not merely about having less but about being more—more present, more appreciative, and more connected to the essence of life.

The Zen and Simplicity stories offer a mosaic of teachings on the value of reducing complexity in our lives and minds. They invite us to reconsider our priorities, to find beauty in the minimal, and to discover the peace that comes from living with intention and simplicity. As we move forward, let these stories serve as a guide, encouraging us to weave the principles of Zen simplicity into the fabric of our daily lives, finding in each moment a deeper sense of peace, clarity, and joy.

"The bamboo that bends is stronger than the oak that resists."

— Japanese proverb

6

Zen and Adaptability

In the ever-flowing river of life, where currents of change constantly reshape the landscape of our existence, the Zen principle of adaptability emerges as a guiding light. This section, 'Zen and Adaptability,' invites us into a contemplative exploration of how flexibility, resilience, and openness to the impermanent nature of life can lead us to deeper wisdom and peace. Through a series of evocative stories, we delve into the essence of adaptability as not just a survival strategy but as a profound spiritual practice rooted in Zen.

Adaptability in Zen is understood as the capacity to flow with life's changes with grace and ease, to stand resilient in the face of adversity, and to embrace the transient nature of all things without attachment or resistance. It is a dance with the unpredictable, a harmonious alignment with the Tao, the way of the universe, which moves and changes in patterns beyond our comprehension.

From the resilience of the willow tree that bends in the storm but does not break, to the serene acceptance of a monk who gives away his cherished robe, the stories within this section embody the strength found in flexibility and the freedom that comes from letting go. They teach us that true adaptability is not a passive surrender to the whims of fate but an active engagement with the present moment, a readiness to meet each situation with a clear mind and an open heart.

As we journey through tales of flowing rivers, bending bamboo, and tea ceremonies embraced by rain, we are reminded that adaptability is an essential quality of the enlightened mind. It is the realization that, in the fluidity of change, there lies the opportunity for growth, creativity, and the unfolding of our true potential.

This introduction to 'Zen and Adaptability' serves as an invitation to view the changes and challenges of our lives through the lens of Zen. As we learn to embrace the impermanence of the world with adaptability and grace, we find ourselves moving closer to a state of balance and peace, where the vicissitudes of life become not obstacles but pathways to deeper understanding and harmony with the cosmos.

Let these stories inspire you to cultivate a spirit of adaptability, to find strength in flexibility, and to discover the profound peace that comes from living in harmonious alignment with the ever-changing tapestry of existence.

THE WILLOW TREE

In a village bordered by a whispering forest and a gentle river, there stood an ancient willow tree. Its branches, long and flexible, danced gracefully with the wind, never resisting, always flowing with the force of the gales that swept through the valley. This willow had witnessed many seasons, its resilience a testament to the wisdom of adaptability.

Nearby lived a Zen monk, Master Hiroshi, who often meditated beneath the willow's expansive canopy. One day, he was joined by a young disciple, Kenji, who was troubled by the recent changes in his life. The stability he had once known seemed to be unraveling, leaving him anxious and resistant to the shifts occurring around him.

Master Hiroshi, sensing Kenji's distress, pointed to the willow and said, "Observe this tree, Kenji. It teaches us the essence of adaptability. When the wind blows fiercely, it bends, but it does not break. By yielding, it remains strong and continues to grow. So too must we learn to adapt to the winds of change in our lives."

Kenji watched the willow, noting how its branches moved in harmony with the wind, neither fighting against it nor breaking under its pressure. "But Master," Kenji asked, "how can I become like the willow? I feel more like a rigid oak that fears it will snap at the first sign of a storm."

Master Hiroshi smiled gently. "The strength of the willow lies not in its branches but in its roots," he explained. "They are deep and spread wide, anchoring the tree firmly to the earth while allowing it to bend with the wind. Similarly, our roots are our values, our practice, and our understanding of the impermanent nature of life. Cultivate these, and you will find the flexibility to face any change with strength and grace."

Kenji spent many days meditating under the willow, reflecting on Master Hiroshi's words. As he deepened his understanding of Zen and the nature of change, he began to see the shifts in his life not as threats but as opportunities for growth and learning. Gradually, his fear and resistance gave way to a sense of peace and adaptability.

"The Willow Tree" is a story of embracing change, a reminder that the true strength lies in our ability to adapt with grace. It teaches us that by cultivating deep roots in our values and

practice, we can learn to dance with the winds of change, growing stronger and more resilient with each passing storm.

THE MONK'S NEW ROBE

In a small monastery nestled among rolling hills and whispering pines, there lived a monk named Daichi. Daichi had been a part of the monastery for many years, his life a testament to the teachings of Zen, particularly those of simplicity and adaptability.

One autumn day, the monastery received a generous donation from a grateful visitor. Among the gifts was a beautiful, finely woven robe, far more luxurious than the simple garments the monks usually wore. The abbot decided that this robe should go to Daichi, who had never sought possessions or accolades but had always served the monastery with humility and dedication.

Daichi accepted the robe with gratitude, aware of the honor bestowed upon him. Yet, as he wore it during his daily activities, he felt a sense of discomfort. The robe was indeed beautiful, but it set him apart from his fellow monks and the simplicity they valued. Daichi realized that the true test of adaptability was not in accepting the robe but in understanding its place in his life of Zen practice.

Not long after, a traveler arrived at the monastery, weary and cold, his clothes tattered from his journey. Daichi, seeing the traveler's need, did not hesitate. He offered the new robe to the traveler, exchanging it for the simple, worn garment the man had been wearing.

Some of the younger monks were puzzled by Daichi's decision. "Why give away such a precious gift?" they asked. Daichi replied, "The robe, like all things, is impermanent. It came to me, and now it has gone to serve another. Our practice teaches us to adapt, not just to the changes in our circumstances but to the needs of others. In giving the robe, I have gained more than I have given."

The story of "The Monk's New Robe" spread through the monastery, becoming a lesson in the true nature of adaptability and the freedom found in non-attachment. Daichi's act of giving was a demonstration of his understanding that the essence of Zen adaptability lies not in clinging to comfort or status but in responding to the moment with compassion and openness.

"The Monk's New Robe" teaches us that adaptability is an expression of deep understanding and compassion. It reminds us that by letting go and responding to the needs of the present moment, we embody the fluid nature of life itself, finding peace and fulfillment in the ever-changing tapestry of existence.

THE FLOWING RIVER

In a verdant valley through which a vibrant river flowed, there was a small village that had lived in harmony with the river for generations. The river provided for the villagers in countless ways, but it was also unpredictable, changing course with the seasons, sometimes providing bountiful harvests and at other times, challenging the villagers with floods or droughts.

One year, the river began to shift its course more dramatically than ever before, threatening to bypass the village entirely. The villagers were anxious, fearing the loss of their lifeline. They convened with the village elder, a wise woman named Keiko, who had always guided them with her deep understanding of the Zen way.

Keiko listened to their concerns and suggested they consult with a Zen monk, Master Daichi, who lived in a nearby monastery. Known for his insight into the nature of change and adaptability, Master Daichi was often sought out for guidance.

When the villagers explained their predicament, Master Daichi smiled and invited them to walk with him to the river. Standing on its banks, he said, "Observe the river. It does not resist change; it flows, always adapting to the contours of the earth. Like the river, we too must learn to adapt, to embrace the flow of life with all its changes."

Inspired by Master Daichi's words, the villagers decided to work with the river's new course. Rather than trying to control or redirect it back to its old path, they adapted their farming practices, irrigation techniques, and even the location of their village to align with the river's flow.

Over time, the village not only survived but thrived, discovering new resources and opportunities that the changed river brought. The villagers learned to see the river's unpredictability not as a threat but as a natural part of life's ebb and flow, teaching them the importance of adaptability, resilience, and the strength found in yielding to change.

"The Flowing River" is a story of embracing change and finding harmony in adaptability. It reminds us that life, like the river, is ever-changing, and our ability to flow with these changes, to adapt with wisdom and grace, is key to finding balance and peace. Through the wisdom of Master Daichi and the actions of the villagers, we learn that in the heart of change lies the opportunity for growth, renewal, and deeper understanding.

THE BAMBOO GROVE

In a monastery surrounded by ancient forests, there was a lush grove of bamboo that swayed with an almost musical grace. The bamboo stood tall, yet bent with the wind, never breaking, no matter how fierce the storm. This grove was a place of reflection for a Zen master known as Kensei, who often brought his disciples there to teach them about the nature of life and the virtue of adaptability.

One particularly stormy day, Kensei led a young disciple, Taro, to the grove. The wind was howling, a powerful force that seemed capable of uprooting even the sturdiest of trees. Yet, the bamboo merely danced, bending to the ground only to rise again.

"Observe the bamboo, Taro," Kensei said. "See how it bends with the wind? It knows that to resist is to break. By yielding, it survives the storm, and it is stronger for it."

Taro watched, mesmerized by the bamboo's resilience. He thought of the challenges he faced in his own life, the times he had tried to stand firm against the forces that sought to bend him. "Master, how can I learn to be like the bamboo? To bend but not break?"

Kensei smiled, placing a hand on Taro's shoulder. "It begins with understanding that the essence of adaptability is not weakness but strength. It is the strength to know when to yield and when to stand tall, the wisdom to recognize that the only constant in life is change."

"In your practice," Kensei continued, "embrace each moment as it comes, without attachment to how things 'should' be. Let the principle of adaptability be your guide, not just in facing the storms of life but in every moment of existence."

Inspired by the bamboo and Kensei's teachings, Taro began to apply the lessons of adaptability to his daily life. He learned to approach challenges with flexibility, to see the value in bending with the circumstances rather than resisting them. Over time, Taro found that he could face life's storms with a newfound resilience, his spirit unbroken, much like the bamboo in the grove.

"The Bamboo Grove" is a story of resilience, flexibility, and the power of adaptability. It teaches us that in the face of life's inevitable changes and challenges, there is strength in flexibility, wisdom in yielding, and growth in the acceptance of impermanence. Like the bamboo, we too can learn to dance with the winds of change, emerging from each storm stronger and more rooted in the wisdom of adaptability.

THE STONE BRIDGE

In a region where the mountains stretched to meet the sky, a river wound its way through the valleys, a lifeline to the villages that dotted its banks. Over this river, there was an ancient stone bridge, built centuries ago by artisans whose names had long been forgotten. The bridge had stood the test of time, its stones smoothed by the relentless flow of the river, yet it remained steadfast, connecting the two halves of the largest village.

A Zen master named Hayato lived in this village, often seen walking across the bridge at dawn, deep in contemplation. One day, while crossing the bridge, he was stopped by a group of villagers who were debating the need to replace the old bridge with a modern one. They were concerned that the ancient structure could not withstand much longer, especially with the recent increase in floods.

Hayato listened to their concerns and then asked, "Have you noticed how the stones of this bridge have been shaped by the river? Each stone, once rough and jagged, has been smoothed over time, adapting to the force of the water. Yet, together, they stand strong, providing a path across the river. There is wisdom in this bridge — the wisdom of adaptability."

The villagers fell silent, contemplating Hayato's words. He continued, "This bridge teaches us that true strength lies not in resistance but in the ability to adapt. Like these stones, we are shaped by the experiences of our lives, smoothed by the challenges we face. And when we come together, supporting one another, we create a path that can withstand the tests of time."

Moved by Hayato's insight, the villagers decided to preserve the stone bridge, reinforcing its structure rather than replacing it. They worked together, each contributing what they could, their efforts a testament to the community's resilience and adaptability.

Years passed, and the bridge continued to serve as a vital link for the village, its smoothed stones a reminder of the wisdom Hayato had shared. The villagers learned to see the bridge not just as a means to cross the river but as a symbol of their ability to adapt and thrive in the face of life's constant changes.

"The Stone Bridge" is a story of resilience, community, and the power of adaptability. It reminds us that, like the stones of the bridge, we are shaped by our experiences, our edges smoothed by the challenges we overcome. Together, as a community, we can stand strong against the flow of time, our adaptability a bridge to a future where we thrive in harmony with the changing world around us.

THE TEA CEREMONY IN THE RAIN

In a quiet corner of Kyoto, where ancient traditions breathed life into the stones and trees, there lived a tea master named Emiko. Emiko was renowned for her tea ceremonies, an art she practiced with the precision and grace of a Zen master. Her garden was a haven of tranquility, the perfect setting for the sacred ritual of tea.

One autumn afternoon, as she prepared for a tea ceremony to honor the changing seasons, dark clouds gathered overhead. Emiko had planned every detail with care, hoping to offer her guests a moment of harmony and reflection. However, as the ceremony began, rain started to fall, gently at first, then with a relentless intensity that threatened to drown the delicate sounds of the gathering.

Emiko's guests looked to her, expecting disappointment or frustration to cloud her serene expression. Instead, they saw a smile of profound peace. Without hesitation, Emiko adapted the ceremony to the rhythm of the rain. She invited her guests to listen to the patter of raindrops as part of the experience, a natural symphony to accompany the whisper of the boiling water and the soft clink of ceramics.

"The rain," Emiko said, "reminds us of the beauty of adaptability. Just as the tea leaves unfold in hot water, revealing their essence, so too must we open ourselves to the unexpected, finding peace and joy in the midst of change."

The ceremony continued, transformed by the rain into an experience of unparalleled beauty and depth. The guests found themselves enchanted, the rain no longer a disruption but an integral part of the ceremony's magic. They sipped their tea, not just tasting its flavor but feeling the essence of life itself — transient, ever-changing, and beautiful.

"The Tea Ceremony in the Rain" is a story about embracing the unforeseen with grace and flexibility. Emiko teaches us that adaptability does not mean sacrificing tradition or precision but finding the space within those structures to flow with life's unpredictability. Her ability to incorporate the rain into the tea ceremony serves as a metaphor for life, reminding us that true harmony comes from our capacity to blend the planned with the unplanned, to dance with the rain rather than waiting for the storm to pass.

REFLECTION ON LESSONS LEARNED FROM ZEN AND ADAPTABILITY

EMBRACING CHANGE AS NATURAL AND NECESSARY

The stories collectively underscore the inevitability and necessity of change in the natural world and our lives. "The Flowing River" and "The Bamboo Grove" remind us that adaptability is not about resisting change but about moving with it, finding strength in flexibility and resilience in the face of life's constant flux.

THE STRENGTH IN FLEXIBILITY

"The Willow Tree" and "The Bamboo Grove" illustrate the strength that comes from flexibility, a counterintuitive concept in a world that often equates strength with rigidity. These narratives teach us that true strength lies in our ability to bend without breaking, to remain rooted while swaying with the winds of change.

MINDFULNESS AND PRESENCE IN ADAPTABILITY

Adaptability is deeply connected to mindfulness and presence. "The Tea Ceremony in the Rain" shows that being fully present allows us to respond creatively and fluidly to unexpected situations. Emiko's ability to incorporate the rain into her tea ceremony highlights how adaptability thrives on mindfulness, transforming potential disruptions into opportunities for beauty and connection.

THE ROLE OF NON-ATTACHMENT

"The Monk's New Robe" explores the role of non-attachment in adaptability. By giving away his new robe to someone in need, the monk demonstrates that our ability to adapt is often hindered by our attachments. Letting go, a core Zen practice, is shown to be essential for true adaptability, allowing us to respond to the needs of the moment with generosity and compassion.

ADAPTABILITY AS A PATH TO INNER PEACE

Across all stories, adaptability is presented not just as a survival strategy but as a path to inner peace and enlightenment. By embracing the impermanent nature of life, we open ourselves to the flow of existence, finding peace in the acceptance of change and joy in the dance of adaptation.

COMMUNITY AND COLLECTIVE ADAPTABILITY

Finally, "The Flowing River" emphasizes the importance of collective adaptability. The villagers' response to the changing river course illustrates that adaptability is also a communal endeavor, where working together in harmony with nature and each other leads to growth, resilience, and shared well-being.

"Adopt the pace of nature: her secret is patience."

— Ralph Waldo Emerson

7

Zen and Patience

In the serene expanse of Zen practice, where each moment is an opportunity for awakening, the virtue of patience shines as a guiding star. 'Zen and Patience' opens a window into the tranquil yet vibrant world of Zen, inviting us to explore patience not just as a virtue but as a profound spiritual practice. Through a series of thoughtfully curated stories, we journey into the heart of patience, discovering its power to transform our understanding of time, our reactions to the world, and our path to enlightenment.

In Zen, patience is understood as much more than the ability to wait. It is a deep acceptance of the present moment, a recognition of the perfection in the unfolding of time, and a commitment to act with mindfulness and compassion, regardless of the circumstances. Patience in Zen is the soil in which wisdom and peace grow, nurtured by the steady rain of mindful awareness and the warm sunlight of compassion.

The stories within this section—from the tale of a monk who plants a barren tree, believing in its potential to bloom, to the narrative of a Zen master who teaches the value of patience through the slow repair of a broken vase—each story illuminates the multifaceted nature of patience. They reveal that true patience is an active engagement with life, a way of being that embraces the delays, the uncertainties, and even the sufferings of existence with equanimity and grace.

As we navigate these narratives, we are invited to see patience not as a passive resignation but as a dynamic force of transformation. It is the quiet strength that enables us to face life's challenges without losing our peace, the enduring calm that allows us to see beyond the immediate to the eternal, and the loving acceptance that empowers us to act with kindness and wisdom, even in the face of adversity.

This introduction to 'Zen and Patience' is both an invitation and a challenge—a call to embrace the slow, the subtle, and the sometimes difficult aspects of our journey with an open heart and a patient spirit. As we delve into the stories that follow, may we find within them the seeds of patience that can blossom into a deeper understanding of ourselves and the world, guiding us toward a life of greater peace, fulfillment, and enlightenment.

Let us walk this path of patience together, discovering how, in the quiet space of waiting and being, lies the profound beauty and wisdom of Zen.

THE SEED THAT WOULD NOT GROW

In a small monastery nestled in the heart of a lush forest, there lived an old Zen monk named Amano. Known for his deep wisdom and serene composure, Amano was revered by all. One spring, he decided to plant a garden within the monastery grounds, intending to teach the younger monks about the virtues of patience, care, and the mysterious ways of nature.

Among the seeds Amano planted was one that held a special significance — a rare flower seed, said to bloom only once in a decade. Day after day, Amano tended to the garden, watering the seeds, nurturing the soil, and ensuring each plant received the care it needed. While the other seeds gradually sprouted and grew, the rare seed showed no signs of life.

Months passed, and the monastery's garden flourished, a vibrant testament to Amano's dedication and care. Yet, the patch of earth where the rare seed had been planted remained barren. The younger monks, curious and somewhat impatient, questioned Amano, "Why do you continue to care for a seed that shows no sign of growth? Is it not futile?"

Amano smiled gently, his eyes reflecting a deep, unwavering calm. "Patience," he replied, "is not about waiting for the seed to sprout on our terms but about understanding and respecting the natural timing of all things. This seed, like all beings, has its own rhythm, its own path to growth. Our task is not to question or rush it but to provide care and patience, trusting in its potential to bloom in its own time."

Years went by, and the rare seed still did not sprout. Yet, Amano's care for the patch of earth never wavered. He continued his daily ritual, embodying patience and faith in the unseen. Then, one morning, a decade after the seed had been planted, the monastery awoke to a marvel — a single, breathtaking flower had bloomed overnight, its colors vibrant and its fragrance enveloping the entire garden.

The monks gathered around, awestruck by the flower's beauty, realizing the profound lesson it represented. Amano's unwavering patience and care had nurtured not just the garden but the hearts of all who lived in the monastery, teaching them the true essence of growth, faith, and the transformative power of patience.

***"The Seed That Would Not Grow"* is a story that illuminates** the virtue of patience as a practice of deep faith and understanding. It teaches us that the fruits of patience are not always immediate but are often profound, revealing the inherent beauty and potential in all living things when given the time and care they require.

THE LONG ROAD TO THE MOUNTAIN

In a distant land where the sky touched the earth at the horizon, there stood a mountain said to be the dwelling place of enlightenment. Many seekers dreamed of reaching its peak, but the path was long and filled with challenges that tested the spirit and resolve of any who dared to walk it.

Among these seekers was a young man named Kenji, whose heart burned with the desire to find enlightenment. He had heard tales of the mountain and the wisdom it offered, and he set out on his journey with a determination that matched the mountain's height.

The road was indeed long, winding through valleys, forests, and rivers. Kenji faced many trials: days of endless rain, nights so cold they pierced the bone, and paths so treacherous they threatened to end his quest before it truly began. With each step, Kenji's initial zeal was tempered by the harsh realities of his journey.

At times, Kenji wanted to give up, questioning the worth of his pursuit. It was during one such moment of doubt that he met an old monk sitting by the roadside. The monk, sensing Kenji's turmoil, invited him to rest and share his story.

As Kenji spoke, the monk listened quietly, nodding now and then. When Kenji finished, the monk said, "The road to enlightenment is indeed long and filled with hardships. But it is not the mountain that grants wisdom; it is the journey itself. Each step, each challenge, is a lesson in patience, teaching us to embrace the present moment with acceptance and gratitude."

Kenji pondered the monk's words, realizing that his impatience to reach the mountain had blinded him to the beauty and lessons of the path. He saw now that patience was not merely waiting but living fully in each step, understanding that enlightenment was not a destination but a way of being.

With a renewed spirit, Kenji continued his journey, no longer in a rush to reach the end but open to the experiences the road offered. Years passed, and with each step, Kenji found the wisdom he sought, not atop the mountain, but within himself, in the patience, resilience, and compassion he developed along the way.

"The Long Road to the Mountain" is a story of the transformative power of patience on the path to enlightenment. It teaches us that the journey itself is where we find wisdom, that each challenge is an opportunity for growth, and that true enlightenment lies in embracing each moment with patience and an open heart.

THE TEA MASTER'S SILENCE

In the heart of Kyoto, where ancient traditions echo through the streets, there lived a renowned tea master, Eiji. His tea ceremonies were sought after by many, not only for the exquisite tea but for the profound sense of peace they offered. Eiji's mastery lay in his ability to weave silence into the ceremony, a silence that spoke volumes, teaching attendees about the depth of patience and presence.

One day, a young, ambitious tea practitioner, Naoki, challenged Eiji. Naoki boasted of his ability to conduct the fastest tea ceremony without sacrificing the ritual's elegance. He claimed that efficiency was the true mark of mastery and insisted that Eiji's slow, deliberate ceremonies were outdated.

Eiji listened quietly to Naoki's challenge, his face serene. Instead of responding with words, Eiji invited Naoki and the townspeople to a tea ceremony the following day. Curiosity buzzed through Kyoto as everyone wondered how the master would address Naoki's challenge.

As the ceremony began, Eiji moved with deliberate slowness, each motion a study in mindfulness. The attendees watched, their initial impatience melting away into a deep, collective breath. The room was filled with a profound silence, punctuated only by the sounds of Eiji's careful preparations.

Naoki, too, found himself drawn into the quiet depth of the ceremony. The world outside seemed to fall away, leaving only the present moment, where each second held a universe of sensations and experiences. The tea, when it finally came, tasted richer than any he had ever had, its flavor enhanced by the patience and presence that had infused its preparation.

After the ceremony, Naoki approached Eiji, bowing deeply. "Master, I now understand," he said. "The essence of the tea ceremony is not in the speed with which it is conducted but in the patience and presence it cultivates. Your silence has taught me more than words ever could."

Eiji smiled, acknowledging Naoki's realization. "Patience," he said, "is the heart of the tea ceremony, and of life itself. It allows us to truly see, hear, and taste the world around us, to appreciate the beauty in each moment."

"The Tea Master's Silence" is a story that illuminates the virtue of patience through the art of the tea ceremony. It teaches us that true mastery and understanding come not from the speed or efficiency of our actions but from our ability to be fully present and patient with each task, each moment. In the silence of Eiji's ceremony, we find a powerful lesson on the transformative nature of patience, a reminder to slow down and savor the richness of life.

THE ARTIST AND THE STONE

In the outskirts of Kyoto, where the ancient city's hustle gave way to serene landscapes, lived an artist named Sora. Sora was a sculptor of stone, renowned not only for his skill but for the profound spirituality that each piece emanated. His sculptures were more than art; they were meditations on the nature of existence, each curve and line a testament to Sora's deep Zen practice.

One day, Sora embarked on a quest to find the perfect stone for his next creation. He searched through rivers, mountains, and deep forests until he found a massive, unshaped boulder, its raw beauty speaking to him of untold potential. Sora transported the stone to his studio, a simple space surrounded by nature, where the journey of transformation would begin.

Instead of immediately starting to sculpt, Sora did something unusual. He placed the stone in the center of his studio and sat before it in silence, day after day. Visitors to his studio were puzzled by this. They expected to see sparks flying, chisels carving, the artist at work. Instead, they found Sora in a state of deep contemplation, seemingly doing nothing.

Weeks turned into months, and still, Sora sat. He observed the stone from every angle, at different times of the day, under the shifting light of the seasons. He sought not just to see the stone but to understand it, to connect with its essence. Sora believed that within every stone lay a spirit, a unique form waiting to be revealed, and it was his task to uncover it — not through force, but through understanding and patience.

After a year had passed, Sora finally picked up his chisel and hammer. With each strike, he was not just removing stone; he was freeing the form that had revealed itself to him through his patient observation. The process was slow, each movement deliberate and filled with reverence.

When the sculpture was finally unveiled, it was unlike anything anyone had seen. It was as if Sora had not sculpted the stone but had allowed the stone to reveal its true nature. The sculpture seemed to pulse with life, a testament to the patience and deep connection Sora had fostered with the material.

"The Artist and the Stone" is a story that explores the profound patience required in the act of creation. It teaches us that true artistry is not about imposing one's will upon the world but about listening deeply, observing patiently, and allowing the natural course of things to guide our hands. Sora's practice mirrors the Zen approach to life — seeing the beauty in what is, understanding its nature, and acting in harmony with it, revealing the transformative power of patience and presence.

THE MONK AND THE ANT

In a tranquil Zen monastery surrounded by whispering pines and blooming cherry blossoms, there lived a monk named Masato. Known for his profound patience and deep contemplation, Masato spent his days in the monastery's gardens, tending to plants and meditating on the nature of existence.

One sunny afternoon, while Masato was raking the sand in the Zen garden, creating patterns that mirrored the flow of rivers and the shape of mountains, he noticed a small ant struggling to carry a leaf across a stone pathway. The leaf was several times the size of the ant, and the journey across the uneven ground seemed an impossible task.

Masato paused his work and sat down to observe the ant. Time and again, the ant would stumble, its burden causing it to lose balance and veer off course. Yet, each time, the ant would pause, reassess, and begin its journey anew, undeterred by the setbacks.

A novice monk, who had been watching Masato, approached him, curious. "Why do you watch the ant, Master Masato? It seems such a small, insignificant thing."

Masato smiled gently, his eyes still following the ant's determined progress. "To some, it may seem insignificant, but in this ant's struggle, there is a great lesson on patience and perseverance. The ant does not lament its burden or the distance it must travel. It simply continues, adapting to each obstacle, persistent in its effort."

The novice monk sat beside Masato, and together they watched in silence as the ant finally reached the edge of the garden, where the ground was soft and fertile. With one final effort, the ant dragged the leaf into a small hole, disappearing from sight.

"See," Masato said, turning to the novice, "the ant has achieved what it set out to do, not through strength or speed, but through patience and persistence. It teaches us that even the smallest actions, carried out with determination and patience, can lead to the fulfillment of our goals. We must learn to approach our own struggles with the same patience, understanding that each step, no matter how small, brings us closer to our destination."

"The Monk and the Ant" is a story that illustrates the virtue of patience in the face of challenges, both big and small. It reminds us that patience is not passive waiting but an active engagement with life's obstacles, a way of moving through the world with mindfulness, perseverance, and a deep trust in the process of becoming.

THE BROKEN POT

In a serene Zen monastery, where the air was always filled with the scent of incense and the sound of gentle chants, there lived an elderly monk named Yoshida. Yoshida was beloved by all for his wisdom, kindness, and particularly, his patience, which seemed as vast as the ocean.

One day, a novice monk named Hiroki accidentally broke a cherished ceramic pot that had been in the monastery for generations. The pot, beautifully painted with scenes from the life of the Buddha, was a gift from a distant temple and held great sentimental value to the community. Distraught over his mistake, Hiroki brought the shattered pieces to Yoshida, expecting reprimand or disappointment.

Instead, Yoshida greeted Hiroki with a gentle smile. "Come, let us sit," he said, motioning to the garden. As they sat amidst the blooming lotuses, Yoshida began to piece the broken pot together. With each fragment he placed, he shared a story of the monastery's history, of monks who had come and gone, of lessons learned, and of the impermanence of all things.

"See, Hiroki," Yoshida said, holding up a piece of the pot, "each crack, each break, tells a story. Our lives, like this pot, are fragile and easily broken. But it is through these breaks, these moments of falling apart, that we learn the most important lessons."

Over the days that followed, Yoshida and Hiroki worked together to mend the pot using the ancient art of kintsugi, where breaks are repaired with gold, highlighting the beauty in imperfection. The once-broken pot was transformed, its cracks now shimmering lines of gold that told a new story of resilience, healing, and the beauty of embracing our flaws.

When the pot was returned to its place in the monastery, it became a symbol of patience and the beauty that arises from accepting and honoring our imperfections. The monks, inspired by the pot's transformation, saw in it a reflection of their own journeys toward enlightenment—imperfect, challenging, but immeasurably beautiful.

"The Broken Pot" is a story that celebrates the virtue of patience in the face of mistakes and imperfections. It teaches us that patience is not merely about waiting but about seeing the potential for beauty and growth in every moment of breaking and coming together. Through the practice of patience, we learn to embrace our flaws, to mend what is broken with love and care, and to find strength and wisdom in the impermanence of life.

REFLECTION ON LESSONS LEARNED FROM ZEN AND PATIENCE STORIES

PATIENCE AS ACTIVE ENGAGEMENT

The stories collectively underscore that patience in Zen is an active practice rather than passive waiting. "The Monk and the Ant" and "The Long Road to the Mountain" highlight how patience involves a mindful presence and engagement with the process, teaching us to appreciate the journey and find wisdom in each step.

EMBRACING IMPERMANENCE AND CHANGE

Zen stories such as "The Broken Pot" beautifully illustrate the acceptance of impermanence and change as natural states of existence. Through patience, we learn to embrace life's imperfections and transient moments, finding beauty and lessons in the impermanent nature of all things.

GROWTH AND TRANSFORMATION THROUGH PATIENCE

"The Seed That Would Not Grow" teaches us that patience is fundamental to growth and transformation. It reminds us that true development, whether personal or spiritual, unfolds in its own time, requiring our sustained commitment, care, and patience.

THE STRENGTH FOUND IN PATIENCE

Through narratives like "The Tea Master's Silence," we see that patience is a form of strength. It's the quiet power to endure, to persist, and to remain centered and compassionate in the face of adversity or challenge.

PATIENCE AND MINDFULNESS

The stories highlight the deep connection between patience and mindfulness. "The Artist and the Stone" exemplifies how patience fosters a mindful appreciation of the present, allowing us to connect deeply with our actions, the people around us, and the world.

THE COLLECTIVE PRACTICE OF PATIENCE

Finally, these stories suggest that patience is not just an individual virtue but a collective practice. "The Long Road to the Mountain" and "The Broken Pot" show how our patience impacts others, teaching and inspiring a communal spirit of endurance, compassion, and understanding.

"To hold, you must first open your hand.
Let go."

— *LAO TZU*

8

Zen and Letting Go

In the tranquil yet profound path of Zen, the practice of letting go emerges as a cornerstone, inviting us into a space of freedom, peace, and deep understanding. 'Zen and Letting Go' beckons us to explore the liberating power of releasing our grasp on the transient, the impermanent, and the illusory, guiding us toward a state of being that is fully awake to the richness of the present moment. Through a tapestry of stories, we embark on a journey into the heart of letting go, discovering its transformative potential to dissolve barriers to our true nature and enlightenment.

Letting go, in the Zen tradition, is not a passive resignation but an active, mindful process of understanding the nature of our attachments and gently releasing them. It is about seeing through the illusions that bind us, recognizing the fluidity of our experiences, and embracing the impermanence of all things with grace. This practice invites us into a deeper relationship with reality as it is, unclouded by our desires, fears, and preconceptions.

The narratives within this section—from the story of a monk who relinquishes his cherished possession to find freedom, to the tale of a master who teaches the lesson of impermanence through the falling leaves—each illuminate different facets of letting go. They reveal that true letting go involves not just the release of material attachments but the deeper relinquishment of our clinging to identities, outcomes, and the need for control.

As we navigate these stories, we are invited to reflect on our own lives, the places where we hold tightest, and the freedom that awaits us in letting go. We learn that in the space created by release, there is room for new growth, unexpected joy, and a profound sense of peace. Letting go becomes an opening to the infinite possibilities that arise when we live with open hands and an open heart.

This introduction to 'Zen and Letting Go' is an invitation to embrace the practice of release as a path to liberation. As we explore the art of letting go, may we find within these stories the courage to release what no longer serves us, to live with lightness and fluidity, and to step fully into the boundless freedom of our true nature.

Let us journey together through the art of letting go, discovering along the way that the greatest strength lies in the gentle release of all that we cling to, opening ourselves to the beauty and wonder of life, just as it is.

THE MONK AND THE FALLING LEAVES

In a serene Zen monastery surrounded by lush forests, there was a young monk named Ren. Among the many trees in the monastery, one ancient maple stood out for its breathtaking beauty, especially when its leaves turned vibrant shades of red and gold each autumn. Ren found peace and solace under its expansive canopy, and over time, he grew deeply attached to the tree's seasonal display.

As autumn approached one year, Ren watched eagerly as the first leaves began to change color. Day by day, he marveled at the tree's transformation, finding in its beauty a profound sense of joy and tranquility. But as the season progressed, and the leaves began to fall, Ren felt a growing sense of loss and sadness. He wished he could preserve the tree's beauty forever, keep the leaves from falling, and the seasons from changing.

Noticing Ren's distress, the old abbot of the monastery, Master Sato, approached him one cool, breezy morning. "You seem troubled, Ren," Master Sato said, his voice as gentle as the autumn wind. "What weighs so heavily on your heart?"

Ren shared his feelings about the maple tree, expressing his desire to keep the leaves from falling. Master Sato listened quietly, then led Ren to a spot where they could sit and watch the leaves as they fluttered to the ground.

"Observe the leaves, Ren," Master Sato instructed. "See how effortlessly they let go, how gracefully they fall. They do not cling to the branch nor fear the journey downward. Each leaf's fall is a dance with the wind, a part of the natural cycle of life."

Master Sato continued, "In their letting go, the leaves teach us the beauty of release, the peace that comes from accepting the impermanence of all things. Our suffering arises not from change itself but from our resistance to it, our desire to hold onto what must inevitably pass."

As Ren watched the leaves falling, a sense of peace began to replace his sadness. He understood that his attachment to the tree's beauty was a source of his suffering, that true peace lay in embracing change, in letting go.

In the weeks that followed, Ren meditated on the lesson of the falling leaves. He learned to see beauty in each moment, whether it was the vibrant colors of autumn, the bare branches of winter, or the new growth of spring. Through the simple act of letting go, Ren found a deeper connection to the natural world, to the impermanent beauty of life, and to the Zen teachings that guided his path.

"The Monk and The Falling Leaves" is a story about the liberation found in letting go. It reminds us that in accepting the impermanence of life, in releasing our attachments and fears, we open ourselves to the profound peace and beauty that lie in the very essence of existence.

THE RIVER'S LESSON

In a village cradled by the gentle arms of a winding river, there lived a man named Isamu. Isamu's home was close to the riverbank, and over the years, he had grown to love the river deeply. However, the river's unpredictable nature, its ebb and flow, sometimes brought floods that threatened his home and fields. In an attempt to protect his land, Isamu decided to build a dam to control the river's flow.

With determination, Isamu worked day and night, piling stones and timber to tame the river. Yet, no matter how strong he built the dam, the river would eventually break through, its waters reclaiming their path with even greater force. Each failure left Isamu frustrated and exhausted, his efforts to control the river seeming more futile with each passing season.

One day, as Isamu sat by the broken remnants of his latest dam, a Zen monk named Soji happened upon him. Seeing

Isamu's distress, Soji sat beside him, watching the river flow freely once again. "Why do you seek to control the river, Isamu?" Soji asked. "Do you not see that its strength lies in its ability to flow unbounded?"

Isamu shared his fears and frustrations, explaining his desire to protect his home from the floods. Soji listened quietly, then pointed to a tree that bent over the water, its branches moving with the current. "Like the river, life is ever-changing, and its beauty comes from its flow. When we try to control it, we only create suffering for ourselves. Instead, let us learn from the river, embracing change and finding strength in adaptation."

Moved by Soji's words, Isamu spent the following days observing the river, noticing how it carved new paths with grace, how it nourished the land even as it changed it. Inspired, Isamu decided to let go of his need to control the river. Instead, he worked with his neighbors to build elevated homes and create channels that would work with the river's natural flow, not against it.

As the seasons changed, the village flourished in harmony with the river. Isamu found peace, no longer fighting the inevitable changes but welcoming them as opportunities for growth and renewal. The river, once a source of fear, became a teacher, its constant flow a reminder of the beauty found in letting go and trusting the natural course of life.

"The River's Lesson" is a story about the freedom and peace that come from letting go of our need to control. It teaches us that by embracing change and working with the natural flow of life, we can find harmony and resilience in the face of life's uncertainties. Like the river, we too can learn to carve our path with grace, strength, and an open heart.

THE BROKEN BOWL

In a bustling market town where the days were filled with the clamor of voices and the clatter of carts, there lived a woman named Mina. Mina had inherited a beautiful ceramic bowl from her grandmother, a family heirloom painted with delicate cherry blossoms and edged in gold. This bowl was Mina's most cherished possession, a tangible connection to her ancestors and the traditions they held dear.

One evening, as Mina was cleaning the bowl, it slipped from her hands and shattered on the stone floor. The pieces lay scattered, the once flawless surface now a jigsaw of sharp edges and missing fragments. Mina sat among the ruins, heartbroken, feeling as though she had lost a part of her family and herself.

In her despair, Mina sought solace at the local temple, where she met an elderly Zen monk named Hoshin. She told Hoshin of her cherished bowl and the sorrow its loss had brought her. Hoshin listened quietly, his eyes reflecting a deep, serene understanding.

After a moment of silence, Hoshin spoke, "Mina, the bowl was indeed beautiful, and it is natural to feel sorrow for its loss. But the true beauty of the bowl was not in its physical form but in the love and memories it represented. These cannot be shattered."

Hoshin continued, "In Zen, we learn the art of letting go, not to diminish our love or memories but to free ourselves from the attachment to physical forms. Your bowl, like all things, was impermanent. Its breaking teaches you the hard lesson of impermanence and the freedom that comes with letting go."

Moved by Hoshin's words, Mina began to see her loss in a new light. She collected the pieces of the bowl and, with Hoshin's guidance, decided to create a mosaic from the fragments. Each piece, though broken, still held the beauty of the cherry blossoms and the warmth of her grandmother's love.

As Mina worked on the mosaic, she realized that by letting go of her attachment to the bowl's original form, she had found a way to honor her memories in a new, vibrant form. The completed mosaic became a testament to the resilience of love and tradition, transcending the fragility of physical objects.

"The Broken Bowl" is a story of loss, impermanence, and the transformative power of letting go. It teaches us that while we may cherish physical reminders of love and heritage, it is in our hearts that these memories are truly kept alive. By letting go of our attachment to material possessions, we open ourselves to new forms of beauty and remembrance, finding peace and freedom in the acceptance of life's impermanence.

THE WEAVER'S LAST TAPESTRY

In a village where the mountains whispered ancient secrets to those who would listen, there lived a weaver named Amaya. Her tapestries were known throughout the land, not just for their beauty but for the stories they told — of love, loss, and the eternal cycle of life. As Amaya grew older, she decided to weave one final tapestry, a culmination of all she had learned and experienced.

Amaya chose her threads with care, each color representing an element of her journey through life. The blues of the rivers that sustained her spirit, the greens of the forests where she found solace, and the golds of the harvests that nourished her body. As she wove, Amaya poured her heart into the tapestry, her movements a meditation on the impermanence of existence.

Word of Amaya's last work spread, and people from far and wide came to see the weaver at her loom. They expected to find her clinging to the threads, sorrowful at the thought of parting with her final creation. Instead, they found Amaya at peace, her face serene, a gentle smile playing on her lips as her hands moved with grace and certainty.

When the tapestry was complete, it was more magnificent than anyone could have imagined. It captured not just the beauty of the world but the depth of human experience, the weaving so intricate that it seemed to pulse with life itself.

On the day of the tapestry's unveiling, the village gathered, expecting Amaya to speak of her attachment to her masterpiece. Instead, Amaya surprised them all by announcing that she would be giving the tapestry away. "This tapestry," she said, "represents my journey, but its true purpose is not to be mine but to be shared. In letting it go, I honor the essence of all that I have loved and lost, and all that I have learned. The beauty of life, like the threads of this tapestry, is woven from moments of holding on and letting go."

The tapestry was given to the village, displayed in the communal hall where all could draw inspiration from its threads. As for Amaya, she found in the act of letting go a freedom that surpassed all she had known. Her final tapestry was not an end but a legacy, a testament to the beauty of life's impermanence.

"The Weaver's Last Tapestry" is a story that explores the art of letting go as an expression of love and gratitude. It teaches us that in the act of releasing, we acknowledge the fleeting nature of our experiences, embracing the cycle of life with open hearts. Through Amaya's journey, we learn that the most profound attachments are not to the creations of our hands but to the love and wisdom we share through them.

THE WEIGHT OF ANGER

In a peaceful Zen monastery set amidst rolling hills and whispering trees, there lived a young monk named Ren. Ren was diligent in his practice, but he harbored a deep-seated anger towards another monk, Jun, who he felt had wronged him. This anger became a heavy burden, clouding Ren's mind during meditation and disturbing his peace.

The abbot of the monastery, Master Hoshin, noticed the change in Ren. One day, he called Ren to walk with him in the monastery's garden. As they walked, Master Hoshin picked up a large, rough stone from the path and handed it to Ren. "Carry this stone with you everywhere for a week," he instructed. "Do not put it down except when absolutely necessary."

Ren was puzzled by the request but agreed. Over the next week, he carried the stone everywhere. Its weight was cumbersome, making even simple tasks difficult. The stone was a constant reminder of the burden he was bearing, but the reason why Master Hoshin had asked this of him remained unclear.

At the end of the week, Ren returned to Master Hoshin, exhausted and eager to be rid of the stone. Master Hoshin asked, "How has carrying this stone affected you?"

"It has been a heavy burden, Master," Ren replied. "It hindered my tasks and my peace of mind."

Master Hoshin nodded. "Like this stone, the anger you carry towards Jun is a burden. It weighs you down, obstructs your path to enlightenment, and disturbs your peace. The time has come to let go of this stone, as well as the anger you hold in your heart."

Ren looked down at the stone, understanding dawning on him. He realized that his anger was a choice, a stone he had picked up and refused to put down. With a deep breath, Ren placed the stone on the ground, feeling a sense of release as he did so.

In the days that followed, Ren worked on letting go of his anger towards Jun. It was not easy, but with Master Hoshin's guidance, he learned to see Jun with compassion and to understand the impermanence of his own emotions. As his anger dissolved, Ren found a deeper sense of peace and clarity in his practice.

"The Weight of Anger" is a story that illustrates the liberating power of letting go of emotional burdens. Through Ren's journey, we learn that holding onto anger is like carrying a heavy stone — it serves only to weigh us down. Letting go is an act of compassion towards ourselves and others, a step towards the lightness and freedom that lies at the heart of Zen practice.

THE LAST LEAF

In a small town nestled between the whispering forests and the serene mountains, there lived an old man named Takeshi. His life was long and filled with both joy and sorrow, and now in his twilight years, he found himself facing his final days with a heart heavy with fear. From his bed, Takeshi could see a single leaf clinging to a branch of the ancient maple tree outside his window. He became fixated on this leaf, believing that his life was somehow tied to it, that as long as the leaf held on, so too would he.

As autumn deepened, the leaf became a symbol of Takeshi's struggle to hold on to life. His family and friends visited, offering comfort and love, but Takeshi's eyes remained on the leaf, his spirit tethered to its fragile presence.

One chilly morning, a Zen monk named Sojun arrived at Takeshi's home. Sojun had heard of Takeshi's plight and sought to offer the peace of Zen teachings in his final days. Sitting beside Takeshi, Sojun noticed the old man's gaze fixed on the leaf outside.

"Why do you watch the leaf so intently?" Sojun asked gently.

Takeshi replied with a weak voice, "That leaf is all that stands between me and the end. I am afraid to let go, afraid of what comes after."

Sojun nodded, understanding Takeshi's fear. "The leaf, like all things, is part of the cycle of life — a cycle of arising and passing away. To cling to it is to suffer, for its nature is to fall when its time comes. Your life, too, is part of this beautiful cycle. To let go is not to lose but to return to the vastness from which we all come."

Takeshi listened, his breath slow and steady. Sojun continued, "In letting go, you find freedom — freedom from fear, freedom from suffering. The leaf does not fear the fall, for it knows it returns to the earth, nourishing the tree that once gave it life."

As the days passed, Sojun's words began to ease Takeshi's fear. He spent his hours in quiet reflection, finding moments of peace and understanding he had not known before. And then, one morning, as the first light of dawn crept across the sky, the last leaf let go, gliding gracefully to the ground.

Takeshi watched it fall, and in that moment, he felt a profound sense of release. A smile graced his lips as he whispered his thanks to the leaf, to Sojun, and to the life he had lived. In letting go, Takeshi found not the end but a return to the source of all things, a gentle rejoining with the cycle of life.

"The Last Leaf" is a story of acceptance, peace, and the beauty of letting go. It teaches us that in the act of releasing, we find our way back to the essence of being, to the interconnectedness of all life. Takeshi's journey reminds us that letting go is not an end but a beginning, a return to the boundless love and peace that is our true nature.

REFLECTION ON LESSONS LEARNED FROM ZEN AND LETTING GO

THE NATURE OF IMPERMANENCE
The stories collectively highlight the impermanent nature of existence, teaching us that clinging to the transient only leads to suffering. "The Monk and The Falling Leaves" beautifully illustrates the cycle of life and the liberation found in embracing change rather than resisting it.

LETTING GO AS LIBERATION
Through narratives like "The River's Lesson" and "The Last Leaf," we learn that letting go is an act of liberation. It frees us from the burdens of clinging and control, allowing us to flow with life's currents and find peace in the acceptance of life's ever-changing nature.

THE POWER OF NON-ATTACHMENT
"The Broken Bowl" and "The Weaver's Last Tapestry" delve into the practice of non-attachment, showing how our attachments to objects, outcomes, and even our creations can hinder our ability to experience life fully. By letting go, we open ourselves to the beauty of the present and the richness of our experiences without the filter of our desires and fears.

TRANSFORMATION THROUGH RELEASE
Each story underscores the transformative power of letting go. Whether it's releasing anger, as in "The Weight of Anger," or facing the ultimate letting go at life's end, as in "The Last Leaf," we see how letting go brings about a profound shift in perspective, leading to growth, understanding, and a deeper connection with the essence of being.

THE PRACTICE OF PATIENCE IN LETTING GO

Letting go is intertwined with the practice of patience. It requires the patience to understand the right moment for release, to sit with discomfort, and to trust in the natural unfolding of life's processes. This patience is a quiet strength that underpins the practice of letting go, offering us a foundation of calm and steadiness in the midst of change.

FINDING JOY AND PEACE IN THE PRESENT

Ultimately, the stories in 'Zen and Letting Go' guide us to find joy and peace in the present moment. By releasing our grasp on the past and our expectations for the future, we open our hearts to the abundance of the now, discovering contentment, gratitude, and a profound sense of well-being in the simplicity of being.

"IF YOU LIGHT A LAMP FOR SOMEBODY,
IT WILL ALSO BRIGHTEN YOUR PATH."

— *BUDDHA*

9

Zen and Gratitude

In the heart of Zen practice lies a profound appreciation for the simplicity and richness of the present moment. 'Zen and Gratitude' invites us on a journey to explore the essence of gratitude, not as a fleeting sentiment but as a fundamental aspect of a mindful and compassionate life. Through a series of reflective stories, we are guided to see the world anew, illuminated by the light of gratitude, revealing the extraordinary in the ordinary, the sacred in the mundane.

Gratitude in Zen is understood as more than just a polite expression of thanks. It is a deep, abiding recognition of the interconnectedness of all things, a heartfelt acknowledgment of the gift of existence. It teaches us to appreciate the abundance of the moment, the impermanence of life, and the beauty of the world around us, even amidst suffering and loss.

The narratives within this section — from the tale of a monk who finds joy in the simplicity of a daily task, to the story of a community that comes together in a moment of gratitude amidst adversity — each illuminate the transformative power of gratitude. These stories reveal that gratitude is not contingent on our circumstances but is a choice, a way of seeing and being in the world that opens our hearts and enriches our lives.

As we delve into these stories, we are invited to cultivate a practice of gratitude, to awaken each day with a sense of wonder and appreciation for the myriad gifts that life offers. We learn that gratitude is a practice of returning to the present, of grounding ourselves in the abundance of the now, and of opening to the joy and peace that come from a grateful heart.

This introduction to 'Zen and Gratitude' is both an invitation and a challenge — to live each moment with a deep sense of gratitude, to transform our relationship with ourselves and the world through the practice of mindful appreciation, and to discover the boundless joy that arises when we truly see the miracle of existence in every breath, every leaf, every smile.

Let us embark on this journey of gratitude together, discovering how this simple yet profound practice can illuminate our path, deepen our connection to the essence of life, and lead us to a place of genuine contentment and peace.

THE MONK'S MORNING TEA

In a small Zen monastery nestled among the verdant hills of a quiet countryside, there lived an elderly monk named Eiji. Each morning, as the first light of dawn broke across the sky, Eiji would begin his day with the simple act of preparing tea. This morning ritual, practiced for decades, had become a profound expression of gratitude for him.

Eiji's tea ceremony was not elaborate nor meant for an audience. It was a quiet, solitary affair that allowed him to connect with the present moment fully. He would start by carefully selecting the tea leaves, each one a gift from the earth, and then heat the water, watching as it came to a gentle boil.

As he poured the hot water over the leaves, Eiji would watch with a sense of wonder as they unfurled, releasing their fragrance into the air. This transformation, so ordinary yet miraculous, filled him with a deep appreciation for the myriad factors that had come together to make this moment possible — the sun, the rain, the soil, and the countless hands that had tended the tea plants.

With the first sip of tea, Eiji would close his eyes, allowing the warmth and the subtle flavors to envelop him. He saw the act of drinking tea not just as a physical nourishment but as a spiritual one, a reminder of the interconnectedness of all life and the importance of being present and grateful for the simple blessings.

One day, a young novice named Kenji observed Eiji's morning tea ritual. Moved by the peace and contentment that seemed to radiate from the old monk, Kenji asked, "Master Eiji, why does this simple act of making tea bring you such joy?"

Eiji opened his eyes, a gentle smile playing on his lips. "Kenji," he replied, "gratitude turns what we have into enough, and more. It transforms denial into acceptance, chaos into order, confusion into clarity. It makes sense of our past, brings peace for today, and creates a vision for tomorrow."

"Through this cup of tea, I am connected to the present, to the world around me, and to the countless beings that contributed to this moment. This awareness, this gratitude, is the foundation of happiness and peace."

Kenji pondered Eiji's words, realizing that gratitude was not about the grand gestures but could be found in the simplest acts of daily life. Inspired by Eiji, he began to cultivate his own practice of gratitude, finding joy and a deep sense of peace in the ordinary moments that he had once overlooked.

"The Monk's Morning Tea" is a story that reminds us of the profound power of gratitude to transform our perception, to enrich our lives with a sense of abundance and connection, and to awaken us to the beauty and wonder of the present moment. Through Eiji's ritual, we learn that every act, no matter how small, can be an expression of gratitude, opening our hearts to the endless gifts of existence.

THE GIFT OF RAIN

In a village nestled at the foot of a sprawling mountain range, the people faced a harsh summer. The sun blazed unforgivingly, the earth cracked under its heat, and the crops withered in the fields. The villagers, their spirits as parched as the land, prayed for rain, but the sky remained clear, an endless expanse of blue.

Among the villagers was a Zen monk named Akira. While the village despaired, Akira moved with a calm assurance, tending to his small garden with care and attention, despite the drought. His actions puzzled the villagers — how could he remain so composed and grateful in such dire times?

One evening, as the villagers gathered to discuss their plight, Akira joined them. He listened quietly as they shared their fears and frustrations. When they turned to him, seeking wisdom or perhaps a shared commiseration, Akira spoke softly, "The rain will come when it is time. Until then, we must see this moment not as a curse but as a gift."

The villagers were taken aback. "A gift?" they echoed incredulously. "How can this drought be seen as anything but a hardship?"

Akira replied, "This challenge teaches us the value of water, the strength of community, and the power of patience. It invites us to be mindful of our consumption, to support one another, and to find joy and gratitude in the simplest of blessings — the coolness of shade, the company of neighbors, the food we still share."

His words stirred something within the villagers. In the face of hardship, they had focused only on what was lacking, overlooking the abundance that remained.

The very next day, as if in answer to Akira's wisdom, dark clouds gathered on the horizon, and soon, rain began to fall — gentle at first, then growing in strength. The villagers stepped out of their homes, faces turned upward, letting the rain wash over them, a baptism of renewal.

As the rain soaked the parched earth, the village came together to repair and replant, their spirits lifted not just by the promise of revived crops but by a newfound appreciation for the gifts that adversity can bring.

"The Gift of Rain" is a story that teaches us about the power of gratitude in the face of challenges. Through Akira's perspective, we learn that gratitude is not dependent on our circumstances but is a choice we can make at any moment. This story reminds us that even in times of drought, there are gifts to be found, lessons to be learned, and reasons for gratitude — if only we have the eyes to see them.

THE EMPTY BOWL

In a modest Zen monastery perched on the edge of a tranquil lake lived a novice monk named Hiro. Despite the serene beauty that surrounded him, Hiro often found himself feeling unfulfilled and longing for more than the simple life the monastery offered. He envied the stories of travelers and the possessions of the wealthy, wondering why his path had led him to a life of such apparent scarcity.

One day, Hiro approached his teacher, Master Sato, with a heavy heart. "Master," he said, "why must our lives be so sparse? Why do we eat the same simple meals every day, and why must my bowl always be empty before it's filled?"

Master Sato listened quietly to Hiro's concerns. The next morning, he invited Hiro to join him for a meal. Before them were two bowls: one was ornately decorated and filled with an array of sumptuous foods, while the other was plain and empty.

"Choose," Master Sato said, gesturing to the bowls.

Hiro, puzzled, chose the empty bowl. Master Sato nodded, and they began to eat in silence. With each bite from his own simple meal, Sato filled Hiro's empty bowl with a small portion, offering a variety of foods from the garden and wild herbs from the forest edge.

As the meal progressed, Hiro realized the empty bowl he had chosen was no longer empty but filled with a meal far richer and varied than any he had imagined. Each bite was a discovery, each flavor a surprise. The simplicity he had once scorned became a source of profound gratitude.

After the meal, Master Sato asked, "Which bowl provided you with more satisfaction?"

Hiro understood then. "The empty bowl, Master," he replied. "It was empty only in appearance but filled with potential. It taught me that our lives, though they may seem sparse, are rich with possibility and abundance. I see now that gratitude does not come from having what we want but from appreciating what we have."

Master Sato smiled, pleased with Hiro's insight. "The empty bowl," he said, "like our lives, holds infinite potential. It is only through gratitude that we can see the abundance that surrounds us, even in simplicity. Gratitude fills the empty spaces, transforming scarcity into sufficiency."

"The Empty Bowl" is a story that illuminates the transformative power of gratitude. Through Hiro's journey, we learn that gratitude is not about the abundance of our possessions but about the way we perceive and value our experiences. This story teaches us that a grateful heart discovers richness in the simplest of things, finding joy and contentment in the potential that lies within the empty spaces of our lives.

THE GRATEFUL GARDENER

In the heart of a bustling city, where nature seemed a rare guest, there was a Zen temple with a small, vibrant garden, lovingly tended by an elderly monk named Keiji. Despite its size, the garden was a haven of peace and beauty, attracting visitors from all walks of life. Keiji, the gardener, was known not only for his green thumb but for his deep sense of gratitude for every plant, rock, and creature within the garden's walls.

One spring day, a curious child named Yumi visited the garden. She was drawn to Keiji, watching him as he moved from plant to plant with a gentle touch and a smile on his face. Yumi noticed that even when he pulled weeds or disposed of dead leaves, he did so with a sense of care and thankfulness.

"Why do you thank the plants, even when you remove them?" Yumi asked, her curiosity piqued.

Keiji looked up, his eyes twinkling with kindness. "Every part of this garden contributes to its beauty and balance," he explained. "The weeds remind us of the wildness that lies just beyond our control. The fallen leaves nourish the soil. Even in their passing, they give life to the new. For this, I am grateful."

Yumi pondered Keiji's words, looking around at the garden with new eyes. She saw not just the colors and shapes but the intricate web of life that each element supported.

"Gratitude," Keiji continued, "is like water for the soul. It nourishes us, helping us grow and flourish. When we appreciate even the smallest things, our world becomes richer, and we understand our place within it more deeply."

Inspired by Keiji, Yumi began to visit the garden regularly, learning to tend the plants and to see the beauty in the cycle of life and growth. With Keiji's guidance, she learned that gratitude was not just a feeling but a way of being, a practice that could transform the way one saw the world.

Years passed, and Yumi grew into a young woman. The lessons of the garden stayed with her, shaping her path. She became an advocate for nature, teaching others about the importance of gratitude and care for the environment.

"The Grateful Gardener" is a story that reminds us of the profound impact of gratitude on our perception of the world. Through Keiji and Yumi's journey, we learn that gratitude is the heart of a mindful life, turning every act into an opportunity for connection and appreciation. This story teaches us that by cultivating gratitude, we can find joy and fulfillment in the simple act of caring for the world around us, recognizing the interdependence of all life.

THE TRANSFORMATION OF ANGER

In a quiet village shadowed by the presence of an ancient Zen monastery, there lived a young man named Taro. Taro was known among the villagers for his quick temper and frequent outbursts of anger, which often left him feeling isolated and full of regret. Despite his best efforts, Taro found it difficult to let go of his anger, which seemed to cloud his view of the world.

One day, after a particularly heated argument that left him feeling exhausted and alone, Taro sought the counsel of the old Zen master, Kenshin, who lived in the monastery. Kenshin was revered not only for his wisdom but for his unwavering sense of calm and the deep gratitude he expressed for all aspects of life.

Taro approached Kenshin with a heavy heart, confessing his struggles and seeking a way to overcome his anger. Kenshin listened intently, nodding thoughtfully before speaking. "Anger," he began, "is like holding onto a hot coal with the intent of throwing it at someone else; you are the one who gets burned. But when we transform our anger through gratitude, we find a path to peace."

Kenshin proposed a practice to Taro. For the next month, he was to keep a journal, not of the moments that sparked his anger, but of the moments, however small, for which he felt grateful. Taro was skeptical but agreed to the challenge.

As the days passed, Taro's journal began to fill. At first, it was difficult for him to find moments of gratitude, but gradually, as he shifted his focus, he began to notice the beauty in the world around him—the warmth of the sun on his face, the laughter of children playing in the village square, the quiet companionship of an old friend.

With each entry, Taro's perspective began to change. He found himself less reactive, more reflective. The anger that had once consumed him started to diminish, replaced by a sense of peace and a deepening gratitude for the life he lived, imperfections and all.

When the month was over, Taro returned to Kenshin, a changed man. He shared his journal, his voice filled with emotion as he recounted the transformation he had experienced. "I realize now," Taro said, "that gratitude is the antidote to anger. By focusing on the gifts of each moment, I have found a way to let go of my anger and embrace a life of peace."

"The Transformation of Anger" is a story of healing and growth, illustrating the powerful role gratitude can play in transforming our inner landscape. Taro's journey from anger to gratitude teaches us that by choosing to focus on the abundance in our lives, we can dissolve the barriers to our happiness, fostering a sense of connection, peace, and profound gratitude for the journey of life itself

THE FEAST OF GRATITUDE

In the heart of a sprawling city, amidst the cacophony of daily life, there existed a small Zen community known for its serene garden and humble temple. The community, though modest, was a beacon of peace for those who sought refuge from the relentless pace of the outside world.

One year, as the season of harvest approached, the community found itself facing unforeseen hardship. A series of unexpected events had left their pantry nearly empty, and resources were scarce. Despite this, the abbot of the temple, Master Koji, proposed that they hold a feast — not one of abundance, but a feast of gratitude.

The community members were perplexed. "How can we hold a feast when we have so little?" they asked.

Master Koji smiled gently. "Gratitude," he explained, "is not about the abundance of what we have but about the appreciation of what we are given, no matter how small. Let us each bring what we can, even if it is but a single grain of rice, and share a meal in gratitude for the blessings we do have."

Moved by Master Koji's words, each member of the community set out to contribute what they could. Some brought vegetables from their small gardens, others brought herbs, and some brought nothing more than a handful of rice or beans. Together, they prepared the meal, each ingredient a testament to the collective effort and goodwill of the community.

As they gathered to share the feast, the air was filled with a sense of unity and joy. The meal was simple, but each bite was savored with a deep appreciation for the hands that had contributed to its creation. The community members shared stories of gratitude, recounting moments of kindness and connection that had touched their lives.

Master Koji spoke as the meal came to a close, "Tonight, we have shared more than food. We have shared the essence of gratitude, which has the power to transform scarcity into sufficiency, sorrow into joy. Let this feast remind us that gratitude is the heart of a fulfilled life, cultivating a sense of abundance that transcends material possessions."

The Feast of Gratitude became a cherished tradition within the community, a yearly reminder of the transformative power of gratitude. It taught them that even in times of hardship, there is always something to be grateful for, and that by coming together in a spirit of appreciation, they could create a sense of abundance that nourished not only the body but the soul.

"The Feast of Gratitude" is a story that celebrates the profound impact of gratitude on our sense of community and well-being. It illustrates how gratitude can turn even the simplest meal into a feast of abundance, highlighting the beauty of coming together to share and appreciate the many blessings life offers, even in the face of adversity.

REFLECTION ON LESSONS LEARNED FROM ZEN AND GRATITUDE

GRATITUDE AS A PRACTICE OF PRESENCE

The stories collectively illustrate that gratitude is deeply intertwined with the practice of being fully present. "The Monk's Morning Tea" teaches us that even the simplest daily routines can become profound expressions of gratitude when we engage with them mindfully, appreciating the miracle of the moment.

THE TRANSFORMATIVE POWER OF GRATITUDE

Through narratives like "The Transformation of Anger," we learn that gratitude has the power to transform our inner landscape, turning feelings of anger, resentment, or dissatisfaction into opportunities for growth, understanding, and peace. Gratitude allows us to view our experiences through a lens of abundance rather than lack.

GRATITUDE IN TIMES OF HARDSHIP

"The Gift of Rain" and "The Feast of Gratitude" show that gratitude is not contingent on our external circumstances but is a choice we can make even in times of difficulty. These stories remind us that gratitude can illuminate the gifts within life's challenges, fostering resilience and a deeper appreciation for life's blessings, no matter how small.

THE INTERCONNECTEDNESS OF LIFE

Stories such as "The Grateful Gardener" highlight gratitude's role in recognizing the interconnectedness of all life. This awareness fosters a sense of stewardship and care for the world, reminding us that gratitude extends beyond personal gain to encompass a deep appreciation for the web of life that sustains us.

LETTING GO AND GRATITUDE

The practice of gratitude is shown to be intricately linked with the art of letting go. By embracing gratitude, we release our grip on what we think life should be, opening ourselves to the beauty and richness of what is. This letting go is not about loss but about finding freedom and contentment in the present.

CULTIVATING A HEART OF GRATITUDE

Finally, these stories underscore that gratitude is a cultivated practice. It requires intentionality and awareness to see beyond our immediate desires and recognize the abundance that surrounds us. Like the Zen practice of meditation, gratitude is a discipline of the heart and mind, leading to a life marked by joy, compassion, and a profound sense of fulfillment.

"Enlightenment, for a wave in the ocean, is the moment the wave realizes it is water."

— Thich Nhat Hanh

10

Zen and Connection

In the journey through Zen, we arrive at a profound realization: that the essence of our being is not separate but deeply intertwined with the fabric of all existence. "Zen and Connection" explores this realization, inviting us to see beyond the illusion of isolation and recognize the intricate web of interconnectedness that binds us to each other, to nature, and to the universe itself. This final section of our exploration into Zen wisdom offers tales and teachings that illuminate the inherent unity of all things, guiding us towards a deeper understanding of our place in the cosmos.

Within the Zen tradition, connection is understood not merely as a philosophical concept but as a lived experience, a fundamental truth revealed through mindful practice and compassionate living. Each moment, each breath, each interaction offers an opportunity to witness and participate in the dance of interdependence that characterizes the natural world and our human existence within it.

The tales in this section — from "The Web of the Spider" to "The Circle of Life" — serve as parables for the myriad ways our lives are connected. They remind us that we are like threads in a vast tapestry, each contributing to the whole's beauty and integrity. These stories invite us to contemplate the spider's web, the forest and its trees, the ocean's waves, the flight of birds, the echo of mountains, and the eternal cycle of life, revealing the profound connections that define and enrich our existence.

Through "Zen and Connection," we are encouraged to embrace a broader perspective, one that acknowledges our shared destiny with all living beings and recognizes the responsibility that comes with this understanding. It calls us to live with awareness, compassion, and gratitude, fostering a sense of kinship with the world that transcends the boundaries of self.

As we conclude our journey through the principles of Zen, let this exploration of connection inspire us to live more consciously, more lovingly, and more harmoniously, aware of the threads that connect us and the impact of our thoughts, words, and actions on the web of life. May we carry forward the lessons of interconnectedness, weaving them into the fabric of our daily lives, and in doing so, contribute to a world that reflects the unity and compassion at the heart of Zen.

"Zen and Connection" is not just a conclusion but an invitation to begin anew, with eyes open to the interconnectedness that surrounds us and hearts open to the profound unity of existence. Let us step into the world with a renewed commitment to live in harmony with all beings, guided by the wisdom of Zen and the knowledge that in connection, we find our truest selves.

THE WEB OF THE SPIDER

In a tranquil corner of a Zen monastery's garden, where the air was always filled with the scent of blooming flowers and the gentle hum of life, there lived an old, wise spider. This spider

ZEN AND CONNECTION

had woven a magnificent web between the boughs of a cherry blossom tree, crafting it with such care and precision that it seemed almost ethereal.

One misty morning, as the first rays of sunlight pierced through the fog, a young monk named Daichi stumbled upon the spider's web. Mesmerized by the dewdrops sparkling on the delicate strands, he observed the web in silent awe, noting how each thread connected to another, forming a perfect harmony of strength and beauty.

As Daichi stood there, the old spider emerged from the shadows, its movements slow and deliberate. "You admire my web," it seemed to say, not through words but through the peaceful energy it exuded.

"Yes," Daichi replied softly, aware of the spider's presence. "It's beautiful. But more than that, it's a marvel of connection. Each strand relies on the others, each supports the whole."

The spider paused, as if contemplating Daichi's words. Then, with a grace that belied its simple nature, it began to weave anew, adding to the web with each precise movement. Daichi watched, entranced by the dance of creation and connection.

After a moment, the spider stopped, and the web stood complete once more, even more intricate than before. "Your web," Daichi mused aloud, "is like the web of life itself. Each of us is a strand, connected to others in ways we may not always see. Our actions, like your threads, touch the lives around us, weaving the fabric of our shared existence."

The spider, having imparted its silent wisdom, retreated to the edge of the web, leaving Daichi to his thoughts. The young monk sat by the cherry blossom tree for a long time, reflecting on the lessons of the web. He realized that just as the spider's web depended on the interconnectedness of its strands for its strength and resilience, so too did the human community thrive on the connections between its members.

From that day forward, Daichi approached his interactions with a newfound appreciation for the intricate web of connection that bound him to others and to all living things. He understood that every act of kindness, every word of compassion, every moment of understanding was a thread in the web of life, contributing to a whole that was greater than the sum of its parts.

"The Web of the Spider" is a story that illuminates the Zen teaching of interconnectedness, reminding us of the profound impact our lives have on the world around us. Through the simple yet profound example of the spider's web, we are encouraged to recognize and honor the connections that bind us, weaving a tapestry of life marked by compassion, understanding, and unity.

THE FOREST AND THE TREES

In a sprawling forest that had stood for centuries, its canopy a tapestry of greens against the sky, there lived a solitary oak tree named Anjin. Anjin was ancient, its roots delving deep into the earth, its branches reaching high into the heavens. Though Anjin stood proud and tall, it felt a profound sense of isolation, believing itself to be separate from the forest that surrounded it.

One day, a Zen monk named Hayato, known for his deep connection to the natural world, passed through the forest. He paused to rest in the shade of Anjin's vast canopy and sensed the tree's loneliness.

"O mighty Anjin," Hayato spoke softly, addressing the tree as an old friend, "why do you stand so solemn and apart?"

In the stillness that followed, Anjin conveyed its feelings of separation, of being just one tree among many, disconnected from the forest's collective life.

Hayato smiled, his eyes reflecting the dappled sunlight. "But Anjin, you are not apart from the forest; you are a vital part of it. Your leaves nourish the soil from which you and your brethren draw sustenance. Your branches offer shelter to the creatures that call this forest home. Even the air we breathe is shared, a gift from the forest to the world."

As Hayato spoke, Anjin began to perceive the forest in a new light. It noticed how its roots intertwined with those of its neighbors, how the birds that nested in its branches sang to the entire forest, and how the wind carried its seeds to distant parts of the wood, spreading life.

With this realization, Anjin felt a profound shift in its being. The sense of isolation melted away, replaced by a deep sense of connection to the forest and all its inhabitants. Anjin understood that it was not just a solitary tree but an integral part of a greater whole, its life entwined with the lives of others in a mutual dance of support and sustenance.

Years passed, and the forest grew and changed. Anjin, now fully aware of its connection to the life that surrounded it, thrived as never before. It became a beacon of strength and peace, its branches a haven for life, its presence a reminder of the interconnectedness of all beings.

"The Forest and The Trees" is a story that celebrates the interconnected nature of existence, reminding us that we, like

Anjin, are not isolated entities but part of a vast, living network. Through Anjin's journey from solitude to connection, we are encouraged to recognize and cherish our relationships with the world around us, understanding that in unity, we find strength, harmony, and the true essence of being.

THE OCEAN WAVES

On the edge of a vast ocean, where the water met the sky in an endless embrace, there lived an old fisherman named Isao. Isao had spent a lifetime at sea, riding the waves and listening to the stories they whispered. Though he had witnessed the ocean's many moods, he often pondered the nature of the waves, each so distinct yet part of the vast expanse of water.

One evening, as Isao pulled his boat ashore, a young monk from the nearby Zen temple approached him. The monk, named Kaito, was drawn to the sea, seeking understanding beyond the temple's teachings.

"Old fisherman," Kaito asked, "you have spent your life with the ocean. Tell me, what have you learned from the waves?"

Isao smiled, gesturing for Kaito to sit beside him on the sand. "The waves," he began, "teach us about the nature of being. See how each wave rises and falls, how it exists for a moment, then merges back into the ocean. So it is with us — we rise, we fall, we are individual, yet always part of something greater."

Kaito listened, the ocean's rhythmic roar a soothing backdrop to Isao's words.

"The waves are not separate from the ocean, just as we are not separate from the world around us. Each wave is the ocean itself, expressing its vastness in a form we can see and feel. And like the waves, we are expressions of the universe, connected to all things, even if we appear to stand alone."

As the sun dipped below the horizon, painting the sky in hues of gold and crimson, Isao's words settled in Kaito's heart. He realized that his quest for understanding was not just about seeking knowledge but about recognizing the interconnectedness of existence.

In the days that followed, Kaito returned to the shore, meditating on the ocean's lessons. He saw himself in the waves, separate for a moment but always part of the boundless sea. This realization deepened his practice, teaching him the true meaning of Zen and the interconnectedness of all life.

"The Ocean Waves" is a story that reflects the profound Zen teaching of interconnectedness and impermanence. Through Isao and Kaito's dialogue, we learn that our sense of separation is an illusion. Like the waves of the ocean, we are each a unique expression of the universe, yet intrinsically connected to the vast web of existence. This tale invites us to embrace our place in the world with humility and awe, recognizing that in the ebb and flow of life, we find our true connection to all things.

THE FLOCK OF BIRDS

In the serene expanse of the countryside, where the sky stretched endlessly and the winds whispered the secrets of the universe, there was a large, ancient tree. This tree, known to the locals as Shinrin, was home to a vast flock of birds. Each morning, the flock would take to the sky in a breathtaking display of unity, their movements synchronized in a dance that spoke of an unseen bond.

A Zen monk named Hiroshi, who lived in a modest temple nearby, would often sit under Shinrin at dawn to meditate and observe the birds. Hiroshi was intrigued by the flock's harmony and wondered at the nature of their connection.

One day, as Hiroshi sat in meditation, a traveler named Sora joined him. Captivated by the sight of the birds, Sora asked, "How do they fly together so perfectly, as if of one mind?"

Hiroshi opened his eyes, a gentle smile on his face. "The birds," he replied, "do not think of themselves as separate from the flock. They move with a shared purpose, each aware of the others, each contributing to the direction and rhythm of the whole. Their unity is a reflection of their deep connection, not just to each other, but to the life force that moves through all things."

Sora pondered Hiroshi's words, watching as the birds dipped and soared, their bodies individual but their intent unified. "Is it possible," Sora asked, "for people to achieve such harmony?"

"It is," Hiroshi answered. "When we recognize that we are all connected, that each of us is part of a greater whole, we can move together with a similar harmony. The key lies in letting go of our ego, our sense of separateness, and embracing the interconnectedness of all life. In doing so, we can find a unity of purpose, a compassion for each other that guides our actions and thoughts."

Inspired by the flock of birds and Hiroshi's insights, Sora began to see the world differently. He noticed the interconnectedness in everything — the way the wind moved the grass, the way the river nourished the land, and how each person's life was woven into the fabric of the community.

"The Flock of Birds" is a story that illustrates the Zen principle of interconnectedness and the potential for harmony that exists when we recognize our unity with all things. Through the simple yet profound example of the birds, we are reminded that true connection transcends physical boundaries, inviting us to live with an awareness of our shared existence and to cultivate compassion and understanding in our journey through life.

THE MOUNTAIN ECHO

Deep within a range of towering mountains, where the peaks kissed the clouds, there was a valley renowned for its echoing cliffs. A Zen monastery perched on one of these peaks, a place of solitude and reflection where the monks lived in harmony with the rhythms of nature.

Among the monks was a young novice named Takumi, who, despite his serene surroundings, struggled with feelings of isolation and disconnection. He often wondered if his voice, his actions, truly mattered in the vastness of the world.

One clear morning, the head monk, Master Gensai, took Takumi to a cliff edge overlooking the valley. "Shout something into the valley," Gensai instructed.

Takumi hesitated, then yelled, "Hello!" His voice carried across the valley, and moments later, the echo returned, filling the air with the same greeting.

"Again," said Gensai.

This time, Takumi shouted, "Peace!" and again, the word echoed back, its sound magnified by the valley.

Gensai turned to Takumi, his eyes reflecting the deep blue of the sky. "Do you hear how your voice returns to you, how the valley carries and amplifies your message?"

Takumi nodded, his heart stirring with a dawning realization.

"Like the echo, every thought, word, and action you send out into the world returns to you, magnified," Gensai continued. "Nothing exists in isolation. Our actions ripple through the fabric of existence, touching lives and shaping the world in ways we may never fully know. This is the essence of connection — the understanding that we are all part of a greater whole, and that everything we do matters."

Takumi looked out over the valley, his earlier feelings of isolation replaced by a profound sense of belonging. He understood now that he was not alone, that his presence was an integral part of the tapestry of life, woven into the vast web of existence.

From that day forward, Takumi approached his practice with a new perspective. He saw each act of kindness, each moment of mindfulness, as an echo sent into the valley of the world, knowing it would reverberate and return, contributing to the harmony of the universe.

***"The Mountain Echo"* is a story that beautifully illustrates** the Zen teaching of interconnectedness and the importance of mindful action. Through Takumi's experience, we are reminded that we are never truly alone, that our every action echoes through the lives of others, and that by embracing our connection to the world, we can live with intention, compassion, and a deep sense of purpose.

THE CIRCLE OF LIFE

In a village nestled between the embrace of ancient forests and the sprawling sea, the cycles of life and death were celebrated and honored as part of the great Circle of Life. The villagers, guided by the teachings of Zen, lived with a profound respect for the interconnectedness of all beings, understanding that every end is also a beginning.

Among them was an elderly Zen master named Juro, who had walked the path of life with grace and wisdom. As Juro's final days approached, he gathered the village and his disciples to share one last lesson.

On the eve of his departure, under the boughs of a cherry tree that had witnessed generations of villagers come and go, Juro spoke: "The Circle of Life is the ultimate expression of our interconnectedness. Just as the cherry tree blooms, bears fruit, and sheds its leaves, so too do we experience the seasons of life. Birth, growth, decay, and death are not separate but parts of a single, unending cycle."

Juro gestured to the tree, its branches laden with blossoms that shimmered in the moonlight. "These blossoms will fall, nourishing the earth, and from that same soil, new life will emerge. Our bodies, too, will return to the earth, but our essence continues, touching the lives of those we've loved, those we've taught, and even those we've never met."

The villagers listened, the gentle words of Juro echoing in the stillness, a reminder of the beauty and impermanence of existence.

"As we honor the Circle of Life," Juro continued, "let us do so with gratitude and compassion. Let us cherish each moment, each connection, for they are the threads that weave the fabric of this endless cycle. In recognizing our part in this great Circle, we find peace, for we understand that there is no true separation between us and the universe."

The following day, as the sun rose, casting a golden light over the village, Juro passed peacefully, his final lesson a lasting gift to those he left behind. The cherry blossoms fell like tears, a silent tribute to a life well-lived and a soul reunited with the great expanse of existence.

"The Circle of Life" is a story that encapsulates the essence of Zen and the profound sense of connection that comes from recognizing our place in the universe. Through Juro's teachings, we are reminded that life, in all its forms, is interconnected, each ending a passage to a new beginning. This story invites us to embrace the Circle of Life with open hearts, to live with mindfulness and compassion, and to find joy and peace in the knowledge that we are forever woven into the fabric of all that is.

REFLECTION ON LESSONS LEARNED FROM ZEN AND CONNECTION

THE WEB OF INTERCONNECTEDNESS

The stories collectively illuminate the intricate web of interconnectedness that binds us to each other and to the natural world. "The Web of the Spider" teaches us that, like the threads of a spider's web, our lives are interconnected, each action creating ripples that affect the whole. This interconnectedness invites us to act with mindfulness and compassion, recognizing the impact of our actions on the web of life.

THE HARMONY OF COEXISTENCE

Through "The Forest and The Trees" and "The Flock of Birds," we learn about the harmony that arises from recognizing and embracing our connections with others. These stories teach us that our strength and resilience are amplified when we work in harmony with those around us, much like trees in a forest or birds in a flock, each contributing to the well-being of the whole.

THE IMPERMANENCE OF LIFE

"The Ocean Waves" and "The Circle of Life" reflect on the impermanence of individual existence and the eternal nature of the life cycle. These stories remind us that, while we may rise and fall like waves in the ocean, we are always part of something greater, contributing to the ongoing cycle of life and death, a process that binds us all.

THE ECHO OF OUR ACTIONS

"The Mountain Echo" teaches us that our actions and words send echoes into the world, affecting not just our immediate surroundings but reverberating through the fabric of the universe. This story encourages us to choose our actions and words with care, understanding their potential to create harmony or discord in the interconnected web of existence.

CULTIVATING COMPASSION AND UNDERSTANDING

Across all stories, the theme of compassion and understanding emerges as a natural consequence of recognizing our interconnectedness. By seeing ourselves in others and acknowledging our shared vulnerabilities and dreams, we open our hearts to deeper compassion and empathy, fostering a sense of connection that transcends physical boundaries.

LIVING WITH MINDFULNESS AND GRATITUDE

Finally, these narratives invite us to live with mindfulness and gratitude, appreciating the myriad connections that enrich our lives. By cultivating a deep awareness of our interconnectedness, we learn to cherish each moment and each being as part of the beautiful tapestry of existence, leading to a more fulfilling and compassionate life.

Conclusion

As we reach the conclusion of our exploration into the profound and transformative teachings of Zen, we find ourselves standing at the threshold of a new understanding — a recognition of the timeless wisdom that Zen offers, not just as a philosophy but as a practical guide for living. Through the tales and teachings of Mindfulness, Impermanence, Simplicity, Inner Peace, Gratitude, and Connection, we have journeyed into the heart of Zen, uncovering insights that illuminate the path to a more mindful, compassionate, and fulfilled existence. Each story, each lesson, serves as a beacon, guiding us towards a deeper engagement with the present moment, with ourselves, and with the world around us.

REFLECTING ON LESSONS LEARNED

Our journey has shown us the power of mindfulness in transforming the ordinary into the extraordinary, revealing the richness of the present moment. We have witnessed the beauty and liberation that comes from embracing impermanence, understanding that in the flow of change lies the opportunity for growth and renewal.

The simplicity of Zen has taught us the value of less, guiding us to find contentment and clarity in the essence of what truly matters. Through tales of inner peace, we have learned the importance of cultivating a sanctuary within, a place of calm and stability amidst the storms of life.

Gratitude has emerged as a profound practice, a way of seeing that transforms scarcity into abundance and fosters a deep appreciation for the countless blessings that fill our lives. And in the stories of connection, we have discovered the indelible truth of our interconnectedness, recognizing that we are all threads in the intricate web of existence, bound by our shared humanity and our collective journey through life.

ENCOURAGING INTEGRATION INTO DAILY LIFE

As we close this chapter, the invitation is to carry these lessons forward, to weave the principles of Zen into the fabric of our daily lives. Let mindfulness be your compass, guiding your attention to the richness of the here and now. Embrace impermanence with an open heart, welcoming the ebb and flow of existence with grace. Find beauty in simplicity, and cultivate inner peace as your truest strength.

Let gratitude fill your days, turning each moment into an opportunity for appreciation and joy. And remember the threads that connect us, fostering compassion and understanding in your interactions with others.

A JOURNEY WITHOUT END

The journey through Zen is not one with a final destination but a path that unfolds with each step. As you integrate these principles into your life, you will find that Zen is not separate from the world but deeply embedded within it, in the laughter of friends, the silence of a sunrise, and the simplicity of a single breath.

CONNECTION

May the teachings of Zen inspire you to live with greater awareness, compassion, and connection. May you find in them a source of peace and joy, a light to illuminate your path, and a reminder of the boundless wisdom that resides within you.

We'd Love to Hear Your Thoughts!

Dear Reader,

Thank you for journeying with us through the pages of this book. We hope it has offered you moments of reflection, insight, and serenity. If you've enjoyed your reading experience, we'd be truly grateful if you took a few moments to share your thoughts with a review on Amazon.

Your feedback not only helps us to improve but also assists fellow readers in finding books that can enlighten their paths. Whether it's a simple rating or a few sentences sharing your reflections, each review is deeply appreciated and makes a significant difference.

To leave your feedback:
1. Open the camera app on your phone.
2. Point your mobile device at the appropriate QR code below.
3. The review page will appear in your web browser.

United States   *UK*   *Canada*

Thank you!

Printed in Great Britain
by Amazon